LEVERAGE

—YOUR—

MINDSET

LEVERAGE

—YOUR—

MINDSET

OVERCOME LIMITING BELIEFS AND AMPLIFY YOUR LIFE!
BE LESS STRESSED, HAPPIER, AND MORE MINDFUL!

RICKY KALMON

Published and distributed by:

SOUND WISDOM

P.O. Box 310

Shippensburg, PA 17257-0310

717-530-2122

info@soundwisdom.com

www.soundwisdom.com

ISBN 13 TP: 978-1-64095-216-4

ISBN 13 eBook: 978-1-64095-217-1

ISBN 13 HC: 978-1-64095-252-2

For Worldwide Distribution, Printed in the U.S.A.

6 7 8 9 10 11 / 26 25 24 23 22

DISCLAIMER

It is very important that you understand that the techniques and/ or exercises in this book cannot make you do anything. Your willingness and openness create the momentum and direction you desire. Ricky Kalmon/Kalmon Productions, LLC motivational programs and techniques should not be considered a form of therapy or be used for the treatment of physical, emotional, or medical issues. If expert assistance or counseling is needed, the services of a competent medical professional should always be sought. Neither Ricky Kalmon nor Kalmon Productions, LLC shall be liable for any physical, psychological, emotional, financial, or commercial damages, including but not limited to special, incidental, consequential, or other damages. You are responsible for your own choices, actions, and results.

AUDIO SUPPORT PROGRAM

This book comes with an audio support program for each chapter. Download the Ricky Kalmon app by visiting **rickykalmon.com/app** or scanning the QR code below. Once you download it, you will have access to the Leverage Your Mindset Audio Support Program that I have created exclusively for this book. Use the password **RKMINDSET** to claim this exclusive content. After each chapter, there will be instructions on which audio track to listen to. Please listen only to the track correlated with each day's activities and instructions.

To my incredible wife and two amazing daughters,
who have been my inspiration to be a better
version of myself every day!

CONTENTS

THE ART OF EXCEEDING YOUR OWN EXPECTATIONS

*"Change the way you think
and you will change your world."*

I CAN DO BETTER. Words like these, spoken to yourself, have a greater impact on your performance, results, and overall quality of life than any other outside incentive or motivation. Your Inner Voice is ultimately what enlarges or shrinks the realm of opportunity and impact in which you live and work. This internal script, which draws on your stored images and associations, forms your mindset—the key to a fulfilling life characterized by resilience, productivity, meaningful relationships, and a lack of stress. The problem is, our mindsets can become oversaturated with negative thoughts, stress, and bad habits and become rigid, enabling limiting beliefs to gain a foothold and inhibit our ability to adapt to change or expand our possibilities.

Many of us are not doing *bad* per se, but we could be doing so much *better*. Oftentimes we become so comfortable running on autopilot and developing other areas of our life—our career, our family, our physical fitness, etc.—that we neglect to attend to the most crucial asset of all: our mindset. We allow the noise and overwhelm of daily life to clog our internal storage and slow down our processing, and we stop striving to create a better version of ourselves. Our minds are like computers that require periodic updating as well as to be reset to recover their full storage and functioning capacity. If you want to make the most of your mindset, you have to update your internal software.

> **"If you want to make the most of your mindset, you have to update your internal software.**

I'm Ricky Kalmon, and I show people around the world the power of thought and how to leverage their mindset. The words we say to ourselves and the mental images on which we focus are the most effective tools we will ever know. As the epigraph to this introduction emphasizes, if you change the way you think, you will completely transform your world.

I am a mindset expert, motivational speaker, and professional hypnotist. Please don't be misled by the word "hypnotist." I'm not talking about putting people in trances and controlling their thoughts and actions. Hypnosis is nothing more than entering into a state of relaxation and using suggestions to create the change and results you desire. Cultivating a relaxed state allows you to be more mindful and aware of directing your positive intentions to frame the new reality that you desire. It is just like updating new software on your computer or mobile device. In fact, all hypnosis is self-hypnosis. I actually refer to it as "self-hypnosis meditation." The individual is entirely responsible for guiding themselves to bring awareness and action to their thoughts.

Every person has thoughts and beliefs that either motivate or limit their success. We convince ourselves that we cannot achieve a goal or do better, and those thoughts are programmed into our mindset. Then, before we even attempt to make progress, our mindset reminds us that it's not possible.

The opposite is also true. When we tell ourselves that we can do better or accomplish a goal, our mindset goes to work to motivate us and strengthen both our desire and our belief that the goals and results we want are within our reach.

There is extraordinary potential lying dormant within your own mind. The key to unlocking that potential is personal awareness of your thoughts and beliefs. In the next 14 days, we will take that personal awareness journey together, and you will learn how to update your mind so that it will work with you to improve your performance, achievements, and enjoyment of life.

You started reading this book for one reason: results. Completing this journey of self-awareness will deliver those positive results! This book will show you how to leverage your mindset so that you can overcome limiting beliefs and amplify your life.

You may be asking yourself, "Can I really achieve more personal growth?" The answer is *YES!* We always have the potential to learn new ways to better ourselves. We simply have to open the storage space to download a new internal script. *Leverage Your Mindset* allows us to tap into that potential and amplify our results in all areas of our lives through the power of mindfulness, relaxation, visualization, and self-talk.

Perhaps you have already achieved a certain level of success in your life and are now looking for the best way to take that success to the next level. You might be a leader, CEO, or an entrepreneur trying to instill a deeper awareness of the principles of success in yourself or your team. You might be in the sales or service industry, or you might be a small business owner. The techniques in this book are applicable to everyone, regardless of the goal, task, or result that you desire. They are designed to create a higher level of belief, engagement, and achievement in anything you do.

Do you have the desire to be less stressed and more successful; to grow your business; to be more focused, more driven, more appreciative, and healthier; to overcome changes; and/or to be more in control of your personal and professional life? I guarantee that one or several of these things sparked your interest. Or maybe all them. We all have deep desires, good intentions, and thoughts of success in many areas of our lives. What is holding you back from turning these hopes and thoughts into actions and realized dreams? Mindset!

Mindset is a program that is stored in our subconscious mind. You're already using your subconscious mind in everything you do. Isn't it time to actively partner with it and let it work with you to create the change and improvement you desire? The process is simple, and it doesn't require a great deal of time or effort. There are no specific skills necessary. You have all the equipment required—the only investment you need is your desire to create the change you seek.

Over the course of the next 14 days, you will learn how to exceed your own expectations. Yes, in just two short weeks, you will discover your greatest coach and ally—your mindset—and master the art of using it to dramatically improve your results and your life. When you tap into your thoughts, you remove the ceiling on your potential and open yourself up to limitless possibilities.

Let's get started.

AUDIO SUPPORT PROGRAM

This book comes with an audio support program for each chapter. Download the Ricky Kalmon app by visiting **rickykalmon.com/app**. Once you download it, you will have access to the Leverage Your Mindset Audio Support Program that I have created exclusively for this book. Use the password **RKMINDSET** to claim this exclusive content. After each chapter, there will be instructions on which audio track to listen to. Please listen only to the track correlated with each day's activities and instructions.

WE CREATE OUR REALITY

The outcome of everything we do, or attempt, is predetermined by our thoughts. Our reality is based on our thoughts and beliefs. This is a critical foundational concept.

This is true regardless of what you do. You might be a C-level executive, a department head, or a project manager. Maybe you are a sales professional or a software engineer. You could work in a manufacturing or service facility, or you might be a college or hospital administrator, a teacher, a surgeon or nurse, or a small business owner. Every person creates their own reality…and their own results. They do this with the most powerful tool they have—their mind; more specifically, the thoughts that guide them.

The habitual thoughts that create and frame our reality gain their traction and power from repetition. They are responsible for our experience of fear or confidence, belief or disbelief, and passion or despair in our lives. Our habitual thoughts have intense power. They can be our best friend or our worst enemy. Too often, they are the latter.

Here is how it works. Our thoughts and beliefs are based on our past experiences. They are all part of our conditioning. As a young child, for example, we learned that an iron and a stove are hot. As we grew older, we didn't have to touch them to reinforce that belief. We just knew—it was part of our belief system. The thought was automatic, and we based our actions on it, making sure we didn't touch those hot appliances. Because these ingrained thoughts are automatic, I call them AutoThoughts.

These AutoThoughts apply to everything in our lives. "I'm too shy to speak in front of a group," "I have no willpower," "I'm afraid of heights," and "I'm not influential enough to be a great salesperson" are all examples of AutoThoughts that determine our response…and our outcome. If we believe that we don't have any willpower, we certainly won't go to great lengths to implement changes in our life that require discipline. If we don't think we could possibly speak to a group, we will probably do everything we can to avoid doing so. Applying our internal beliefs to anything in our lives, we can easily see how our thoughts impact our results.

But what would happen if those thoughts and beliefs could change to create the results you really want? They can, but first you have to become aware of those thoughts that are automatically running in your mind. Then, as soon as a negative or limiting thought is triggered, you have to interrupt it—stop it in its tracks and replace it with a thought that is aligned with what you want. This process involves bringing more mindfulness to, and then disturbing the flow of, negative or restrictive thoughts, and then consciously establishing a more productive mental framework, which is why I sometimes refer to it as "Disruptive Awareness."

For example, when you catch yourself thinking, "This is the best I can do. I can't do any better," disrupt that thought and replace it with its counterpart: "I'm going to be great! Today, I'm going to be better and think differently."

It is the AutoThoughts that we repeat in our mind that determine our reality and our results. We can design these habitual thoughts on purpose…or we can allow the world to choose them for us randomly. The choice is ours to make.

Before you make that choice, it will benefit you to know that there are two types of AutoThoughts: constructive and destructive.

Destructive AutoThoughts can be defined as the habitual, automatic thoughts of fear, worry, doubt, and negativity that drag us down and hold us back. These are limiting thoughts. If you believe you cannot do something, your automatic response, your reality, will be based on that belief. Your mind now has faith that your negative thought is valid and true, and your mind acts on that belief. The repetition of negative thoughts becomes the programming, the software, the "app" determining how our mind reacts and creates outcomes. Who really owns AutoThoughts? We do! Can we change destructive AutoThoughts? Yes, absolutely we can!

Constructive AutoThoughts can be defined as the habitual, automatic thoughts that create positive faith and belief in our ability to succeed. These thoughts kick in to create a positive force that repels doubt and negativity and encourages us to find solutions to obstacles and challenges. They can drive us to succeed in something that we envision or trust is possible. It is the constructive thoughts that are repeated in our mind that determine our experience of life and make our best results possible. Consciously choosing and reinforcing constructive AutoThoughts facilitates a positive response from you and those with whom you interact.

We invest in equipment and software to streamline processes and facilitate progress. We continually seek ways to improve production and efficiency. We invest in training to make sure we have adequate knowledge to perform tasks and continue our education to make ourselves more qualified and more knowledgeable. Most people are willing to make those investments, yet they fail to make an investment by updating the most powerful asset they have—their mindset. The thoughts that are loaded into our mindset have the potential to alter the outcome of virtually everything we attempt to do in all areas of our life.

Leverage Your Mindset breaks the norm and creates action to allow you to harness the power of your thoughts to create beneficial change in your life. This goes beyond positive thinking. The process of updating your mindset with constructive AutoThoughts requires awareness and consistent effort. It is more than a change in thinking; it is a lifestyle change, one that is very intentional. This is one of the most effective processes for improving results and enhancing success.

Can we think our way to success? Yes! Studies have shown that positive thoughts actually make us more mentally alert because they stimulate nerve connection growth and increase mental productivity, which improves our ability to think and analyze. It also affects our perspective and response to our environment and the people around us. In addition, programming constructive thoughts into our mindset makes us more attentive, creative, and optimistic.

A study published by *WebMD* details the experience of a group of water polo athletes who included constructive, positive self-talk during the process of learning something new and another group who didn't. The study found that the group who engaged in positive thoughts and self-talk made more improvement than the other group, and they had better focus and concentration.[1]

In this book, I will teach you how to do the same thing so that you can update your mindset—your awareness app—and remove unproductive, limiting thoughts and beliefs. It doesn't take a lot of work; in fact, one of the most important parts of the process is that you have to learn how to relax.

WE ALWAYS HAVE A CHOICE

Let me share something from my own experience that may give you a better sense of how constructive AutoThoughts can dramatically and positively impact the quality of your life. Years ago, a dear friend of mine, Mike, taught me a great life lesson: our minds are the garden of our lives. If we neglect our AutoThoughts, if we do not tend to them consistently like a gardener tending to his garden, our mindset may not be fruitful. If we don't tend to our garden and remove the negative growth, it can stunt any positive growth.

"Our minds are the garden of our lives.

Mike was always a positive role model for me. I admired the contagious sense of joy with which he approached each day, his seemingly inexhaustible ability to make me laugh, and the happiness he brought to everyone with whom he connected in life. I was shaken deeply when I learned that Mike had been diagnosed with lung cancer.

That was a tough time, but Mike seemed to find a way to look on the bright side of what had to be a very dark situation. He taught me that one powerful way human beings can start making conscious choices about the kind of "mental garden" they want to live in is to change their perspective.

One day, I was having a particularly challenging time. It was one of those days when Murphy's Law prevailed—if anything could go wrong, it seemed to find a way to do just that. I was feeling frustrated and distraught, so of course, my focus was on my problems. Then, I saw a picture of Mike and me. Like always, he was smiling in the photo, just like I had seen him smiling when I had last visited him in the hospital.

At that moment, a little voice inside my head said:

You think this was a rough day. You think you've got all these difficult things going on. You think you've got these enormous challenges in your life...but those aren't really problems. Right now, Mike would trade places with you in a heartbeat. He wishes he could have the "problems" that you think you have right now.

My whole outlook on my day—my whole outlook on my life— pivoted at that moment. In an instant, I was more patient, more resourceful, and more focused. Somehow, I had even managed to put Mike's illness in perspective. The moment I took ownership over the "seeds" I was planting in my mental garden, the flowers came.

It's all about the power of suggestion, which can evoke a constructive response to even the most difficult situation.

To flip that switch, I use the principle of constructive Auto-Thoughts to reframe my situation. Here is what that thought sounds like when expressed in words: *Even on my so-called worst days, even when I face what I think are impossible problems, there are people who would happily trade places with me in a second.*

You and I really are in control of our thoughts on a daily basis...if we choose to be. Again: our thoughts can be our best friend or our worst enemy. That is entirely up to us. We are in the driver's seat, and we decide if we are willing to take control of our AutoThoughts.

I am here to coach you and help you assume that control, which is your privilege as a member of the human race. Most individuals never claim that right; they allow other influences to chart their course.

The process of updating your thoughts and your mindset is powerful. It can boost your confidence, help you overcome doubts and fears, break bad habits and create positive ones, and make you more productive and efficient. Done consistently, it will reduce stress and improve your mental and physical well-being. However, the key word is *consistency*. Yes, this is a 14-day process, but the process does not stop there. You can never stop working on yourself. There will always be new challenges and hurdles, along with new opportunities. You must continually update your mindset and the thoughts you feed your subconscious to stay abreast of those challenges and prepare yourself for success when new opportunities present themselves.

IT'S ALL UP TO YOU

Before you go any further in this book, it is important to recognize that *you already have everything you need to make your life a masterpiece.* The question is whether you will choose to *use the resources* you have.

I designed this book with the aim of providing you with these resources, and I wanted to make it easy for you to reference the key concepts whenever you need to do so. However, I can't do everything—if you are going to succeed, you must be committed. You have to take action and be accountable for your results. It is important that you execute the very simple AutoThoughts activities and action steps I share with you along the way. I refer to them as Software Updates and Progressive Jumps, respectively.

The results and success that you will gain from the next 14 days and beyond are up to you. If you *are* ready to take action, if you *are* prepared to tap into the astonishing power of your whole mind, if you *do* want to become your best possible self and begin living life with unlimited potential…please keep going!

SOFTWARE UPDATES

> ❯ The thoughts that guide your actions and results are based on your conditioning, experiences, and beliefs. If

you want to change your actions and results, you have to change your thoughts.

❯ Becoming aware of your automatic thoughts, or AutoThoughts, is the key to creating change and improving your results.

❯ Once you are aware of your destructive AutoThoughts, you need to consciously disrupt them and replace them with constructive AutoThoughts that support the results you want. Along with becoming more intentional about your goals and purpose, this AutoThoughts process is part of updating your mindset, your awareness "app" that frames your experience of life.

PROGRESSIVE JUMPS

❯ Please quickly write down your answer to the question below. Don't read anything into the question; just rapidly fire off the first three answers that come to mind. Are you ready? Great. Let's get started.

- What three habits do you have?
- I repeat: What three habits do you have?
- Again: What three habits do you have?

STOP! Don't continue until you write down your answer to the above question. It is important to follow through with this step before progressing further.

When you have written down your answer, continue reading.

Notice that I asked the same question three times. I did that so that you would focus intently on the question.

Most people misinterpret this question. In fact, when asked this question, 90 percent of my audiences fail to truly listen to it. When I ask them to write down three of their habits, those people write down negative habits. For instance, "I don't exercise enough," "I am not organized," or "I eat too much junk food."

Notice that nowhere in the question did I ask for negative habits. I simply asked for three habits.

This is an enlightening exercise for some people. They realize that they have read something into the question that was not there. They realize that some part of their mind interpreted a habit as being something bad, not good. That is worth noticing. That is an AutoThought at work—a destructive one.

Guess what? Habits can be good. Habits can be great! One habit of professional golfer Phil Mickelson is to make 100 three-foot putts during each practice session. It is easy to see how that habit benefits his game, as he has won 44 events on the PGA Tour, including three Masters Tournaments, a PGA Championship, and an Open Championship. The late NBA superstar Kobe Bryant exemplified the power of habits and a strong work ethic. One of the reasons behind his success on the court is that he woke up at 5:00 A.M. and put up 400 shots every single day without fail. He was always the first person in the gym and practiced for hours before each game he played. These habits sharpened Kobe's technical skills, but more importantly they supported him in the mental game of basketball, conditioning him for success by making it that much easier to stay committed to his training and feel confident in his abilities. Millions of people identify his true mental mindset for greatness on and off the court—as a basketball player, as an entrepreneur, as a teacher and mentor, and as a father. His passing has reminded us to be mindful about how we should spend time focusing on how we can be the best possible version of ourselves in both our professional and personal life.

Good habits can be *any* personal or professional routine that makes us better at *anything* we do. Again, I did not ask about bad habits. I asked about habits. Why do so many of us automatically ascribe negativity to the word *habit*?

The answer lies in our software—in the "app" we have chosen to make our mind work, perhaps without even realizing what we have done. Somewhere in our programming, we changed the use of the word *habit* to identify it exclusively with something negative. Because of the way we typically use the word *habit*, we have given it a negative connotation.

The same is true for other words. "Diet" is a good example. A diet is simply the types of food we eat for nutrition and sustenance. However, when we hear the word *diet*, most of us automatically think of a weight-loss plan—and of food deprivation and hardship.

Why is this important? Because negativity affects how the brain works, and it has a very significant impact on relationships.

Research with corporate teams shows that we need a minimum of three positive thoughts to counter each negative thought or expression. When negative expressions are followed by fewer than three positive thoughts, the relationship is likely to fail. Increase that number to five positive thoughts or expressions, however, and relationships will be on track to flourish. If this is true for the words we say to each other, think about how much impact it has on the thoughts we say to ourselves.

Somewhere along the line we may have installed an "app" that conditioned us to think that habits are, by definition, bad things to have. They are not!

Did your mental "app" do the same thing? Did you write down three positive or negative habits? If the habits you listed were positive, that is great! If they were not, do not feel bad—you are in the majority.

The good news is that you can change the way you think and the habits you don't like. Bad habits can be changed just as easily as changing an "app" that you use (or delete!) on your smartphone.

The next time you and I talk about habits, it will be easier for you to associate a habit with something positive, which is precisely why I included this exercise—to help you see that we often think of ourselves and our abilities in ways that we do not even realize…and that we can change the way we think about things and, by doing so, instantly change our lives for the better.

If you are ready to be challenged, ready to take action, and ready to follow through, you are ready for a 14-day transformation that will show you how you can think your way to success in anything you do.

IMPORTANT: This book is set up as a 14-day plan. The first chapter corresponds with the first day. Ideally, you should complete the chapters in order, starting with the first chapter on Day 1. Then, complete one chapter a day until the program is finished.

> If you have not already downloaded my app, please download it by visiting **rickykalmon.com/app**. Once you download it, you will have access to the Leverage Your Mindset Audio Support Program that I have created exclusively for this book. Use the password **RKMINDSET** to claim this exclusive content. You can now listen to the first track.

MAXIMIZING YOUR MOST VALUABLE ASSET

"Embrace the unfamiliar, and release
yourself from the familiar."

IMAGINE you are in a meeting with a new financial advisor, and as soon as you sit down in their office for your first meeting, you are told to "list your three most valuable assets in rank order."

I'm not a financial expert, but this is also one of the very first questions I ask my clients and program participants. I'm not interested in what stocks they think are winners, what kind of car they drive, or even where they live. But I've found that the answers that lie beyond this one simple question lead to major life and career breakthroughs for those willing to invest the time…and seeing these breakthroughs is one of the most exciting and inspirational things you can witness!

But back to the three-most-valuable-assets question: when I ask participants in my programs this question, the most common responses are "homes," "investment portfolios," and "cars."

Then I ask the kicker: "What investment does it take to keep your top assets consistently performing their best?"

What does this mean? Let's use a car as an example, and let's assume that you have a really nice car—a top-of-the-line, brand-new, high-performance luxury car.

Would you take your car on a trip when it's low on oil and hasn't been in for its regular maintenance appointments? Of course not! Your car is one of your top assets, so you take exceptional care of it, making sure you adhere to the maintenance schedule and perform needed repairs right away. Even the fuel you put in your car should be top grade. High-performance cars require high-dollar expenditures to keep them running their best, and you happily invest your time and money to keep this asset performing at its very best every day.

What about your house? Did you buy the very first one you looked at when you were house hunting? Probably not. More than likely, you put a lot of thought into the features you wanted in your house, knowing which were absolute musts and which were nice-to-haves. You probably knew what type of house would work best for your family. If you have kids, you spent some time researching the school district. You did your due diligence, making sure you weren't sinking your money into a house in a high-crime area. Then you probably spent a good amount of time visiting different houses until you found "the one" that met your needs and your budget.

Once you buy a home, you continue to invest in it. You aren't going to let one of your biggest assets fall into disrepair. You take care of your lawn. You invest in home insurance so if a disaster hits, you are able to repair your asset and continue to build equity.

Would you ever dream of setting up a huge automatic withdrawal from your bank account for investments that you know nothing about? Of course not! If you have an investment portfolio, you have either conducted sustained research into the funds, stocks, bonds, etc., yourself or consulted with an experienced financial advisor before making any purchases. To ensure that you maximize your returns and eventually end up well positioned for retirement, you monitor your portfolio, reinvesting dividends and rebalancing investments as necessary.

Homes, cars, and investments might not be your top three assets, but take a moment right now to identify what your "big three" are. Then, do a quick personal audit and add up all the costs associated with your top three assets. Estimate not only how much money it costs to maintain these assets every year, but also how much time the upkeep requires.

The numbers with which you end up are probably pretty substantial. But guess what? Your most valuable asset isn't written anywhere on that page. In fact, if you are like most people, your most valuable asset isn't getting nearly the attention it requires to yield its very best return. There's a pretty good chance there's an auto-draft draining your most important asset and you don't even know it. Your most valuable personal asset is *you*, and it's time to start investing time and resources into yourself so that you can perform at your very best.

Everywhere we turn, there are reminders about the importance of maintaining our physical health through proper nutrition, frequent exercise, regular visits to the doctor, and getting plenty of rest. And it's true: if our bodies aren't healthy, it's difficult to maximize our performance. But it's just as important to take care of our mindset...how we think has an enormous impact on our ability to create the life we want.

You are your most valuable asset. This means the total you—your physical body and your conscious and subconscious mind. Both elements must be well taken care of to perform at their optimal level. Investing in your most valuable asset—you—will greatly impact the following three aspects of your life in profound ways:

1. **Your mindset.** Your mindset is an invaluable asset with endless possibilities. Like infinity, it has no boundaries. As your internal hard drive, it has a limitless capacity. It can function on what is already there, without requiring further nourishment or attention, or it can continually be exercised and fed new thoughts, suggestions, emotions, and experiences. How we do this is by taking time to relax daily, an investment in ourselves that brings an unlimited return.

2. **Your time.** Your time is the ultimate nonrenewable resource. There is only so much of it, and once it is gone, it is gone forever! How you decide to use the time available to you today and in each of the days that follow will determine the quality of your life. Through the journey of self-discovery you are about to take, you will have the opportunity to unlock hidden secrets to your own success and discover the eye-opening reasons you have

been sabotaging that success. This is a continual growth process, but I know you will begin to see results immediately...if you commit to investing the time to follow and complete this program. Your time is valuable each and every day. Make a 14-day investment right now that will continue to work for you for the rest of your life.

3. **Your decisions.** The decisions you make right now, in the present moment, define you as a person. Think about how much time, effort, and energy you have chosen to devote by analyzing, maintaining, and attending to your physical assets. Now, think of how much attention you have dedicated to enhancing your mindset and bettering your life. Most of us never take true personal time for ourselves. Setting aside daily personal time is a mission-critical investment, a decision you should be able to make in a heartbeat, like deciding to eat or sleep. Once you commit to investing in yourself in this way, you will begin to make decisions that will amplify your life and your success automatically, shifting your default operating system from one of mindlessness, busyness, and fatigue to one of intentionality, presence, and drive.

As you can see, these assets are not material. Perhaps this is one reason that we do not invest in them as often as we should. However, everyone has these assets and the ability to use them to create growth and success in their lives. In this program, we are going to discover how to invest in them to maximize their value and our results. To do that, we need to make our mind a daily priority.

Think of your brain as a computer and your mindset as your personal software. Having the right software installed is critical for quick, streamlined performance, and finding and eradicating viruses that slow down the computer is required to ensure a healthy machine. You know those frequent updates that pop up in your app store that remind you that there is an update ready to be installed? Our mindset requires updating, too, and today's the day you click "Install updates now."

> **"Our mindset requires updating, too, and today's the day you click "Install updates now.""**

So much of our success depends on how we manage our thoughts. Updating our personal software with the right thoughts, as well as weeding out destructive and otherwise unhelpful thoughts, is absolutely life-changing.

Scientific research has proven that disciplining our thoughts to tend toward positivity and success profoundly impacts our lives—in particular, by enabling us to identify additional opportunities. Barbara Fredrickson, a psychology professor at the University of North Carolina at Chapel Hill, calls this the broaden-and-build theory. In case studies, groups were shown videos that produced positive emotions, negative emotions, or neutral emotions. They were then asked what they would do in similar situations. Those who viewed the negative emotion-generating videos had the fewest responses, because they were focused on the emotion, which limits the ability to be aware of anything else. This produces a fight-or-flight instinct, which makes us blind to opportunities. The neutral video viewers listed a few actions they would take, but it was the positive viewers who really proved the theory. They listed considerably more actions they would take if they were in such a situation, lending credibility to the theory that a positive mindset expands our perspective and brings awareness to more options.

Fredrickson's findings reveal that positive thoughts and emotions significantly widen our sense of possibilities. They open up the mind, which, in turn, supports the building of new skills and the ability to identify resources that are available to us. This cannot happen with negative emotions because they are all-consuming and limit our thinking solely to the negative situation and the perceived outcome.[2]

We will go into greater detail about positive thoughts later in this book. For now, be mindful about and disciplined with your thoughts. Notice how often you feed yourself positive thoughts, support, and reinforcement and how often you paralyze yourself with thoughts of fear, anger, or anxiety.

Committing quality time to updating your thoughts—your mindset software—is the first shift you must make in your journey to becoming your absolute best.

I work with top performers in many industries, golfers, NFL and MLB athletes, and CEOs of Fortune 500 conglomerates, and almost always, their first reaction to being asked to carve out time for changing their mindset is to say that they don't have time. A close second is their claim that jumping off the hamster wheel of work and life—even for just 15 minutes a day—will make them lose their edge. I'm here to remind you that you don't have the luxury of failing to prioritize your mindset. If you do not take the time now to maintain your mindset, it will cost you more time later, whether in reduced productivity, missed opportunities, illness, or other consequences of complacency. Moreover, even if you're not presently aware of it, running on fumes is dulling your "edge." To sharpen your mindset and perform at your full creative, athletic, intellectual capacity—you name it—you must periodically update your internal software.

The stakes are larger than you can imagine, so I'm giving you permission to manage your top asset with even more rigor and attention to detail than you do any monetary or material asset. Starting today, treat your mindset just like you would a multimillion-dollar portfolio or complex machine: schedule time to set it up for success, and watch your investment grow and flourish with regular maintenance. Give yourself permission now.

This program is about updating your mindset in order to maximize your most valuable asset—you. It is an absolute necessity that you invest in your mind; if you fail to do so, you will not grow. You will continue to have the same results you've always had—or perhaps worse! Nothing will change for the better.

"Give yourself permission to treat your mindset like the priceless asset it is.

The fact is, the brain requires stimuli in order to function at its optimal level. It's the electronic hub of our body, and it must be fed positive energy in order to perform at its best. Starting today, begin the process of updating your mindset. Leverage Your Mindset is a program designed to help you do that. Other ways you can shift your mindset with little effort include:

Play: By doing something you enjoy, you are feeding your mind with positive emotions and energy, while releasing those that no longer serve you. You are reducing stress and opening yourself up to different experiences and possibilities.

Rest: Everyone needs sleep, but I'm talking about relaxation. This doesn't have to be a two-hour nap, either. A five-minute break, coupled with deep breathing exercises, can have a phenomenal effect on your ability to concentrate and problem-solve. It can also be just as energizing as falling asleep. On Day 2, we will learn how to create this deliberate relaxation in order to maximize our mindset.

Be happy: Most people believe that success creates happiness. *When we finally get where we want to be, we'll be happy. When we finally have the wealth we want, we'll be happy. When we land that* *job or get that promotion, we will finally be happy.* What if it's the other way around, though? I propose that happiness is an ingredient that actually creates success. Focus your mind and attitude on things that make you happy, and I believe you will invite more happiness (and, therefore, success) into your life.

Give me 10 to 15 minutes every single day for the next 14 days, and I'll guide you to updating your mental software—and turbo-charging your life.

SOFTWARE UPDATES

> Change your mental software, change your life.

> You are an asset, and the way you think is either growing that asset or draining it.

> Instead of thinking that achieving a milestone in life will make you happy, choose to be happy first. When you are happy, you're more likely to create success and meet your goals.

PROGRESSIVE JUMPS

> ❯ Build a personal portfolio by asking yourself a few questions; then put your answers where you can refer to them:

> - What makes you unique?
> - What do you bring to the table that makes a difference?
> - In what areas are you an expert?

❯ List ways you can maintain your top asset.

❯ As a reinforcement tool, you can now listen to "Day One" in the audio program.

RELAX

"Your mindset offers you the power to transform your world. Relaxation is the key to harnessing that power."

TODAY, you and I are going to begin learning how you can stop sabotaging your own mind and start positioning yourself for unlimited success. You will do this by attracting positive thoughts and attitudes and gaining the confidence to achieve exactly what you want. That process begins with a simple-sounding step: relaxing.

Contrary to what we've been led to believe, taking swift and decisive action is not the first step in creating change or success. The first step is, in fact, an opposite action—relaxation. You really can replace negativity and doubt with powerful positive beliefs that will instill their corresponding realities in your life. You have all the tools you need to accomplish important professional or personal goals, reduce your stress levels at work or at home, improve your health and wellness, or overcome habits that are not supporting you, but you cannot achieve any of these visions of success without relaxation.

The AutoThoughts process begins with clearing your mind and consciously creating a clean slate so that you can begin to rewrite your own mental "app" and subsequently take control of your mindset. It is important to understand that your mindset—or the part of the mind that the professionals refer to as the "subconscious"—is already programmed. That programming began the day you were born. It knows your past, your fears, and your doubts. Whenever you attempt anything, your conscious mind defers to this deeper part of your brain and retrieves information that is then used to determine whether you will, or will not, succeed. Although this programming of your mental "app" already exists, you have the power to change it RIGHT NOW.

Your subconscious is always working to protect you, which is why it recalls everything that has caused you disappointment, fear, or failure in your life. It brings that information or memory back in relevant situations, reminding you of your failure and the way it made you feel. The response is natural—you doubt that success is possible, you lose confidence in yourself, etc. These internal thoughts are self-sabotaging and pave the road to repeating the same results you've had in the past.

This programming isn't permanent, and that's a great thing. It is always under your control, and it always has been. But there is a catch: to change the programming, you must be willing to change the way you use your mind. You will begin that process today by learning to relax in ways you have not relaxed before...and at a deeper level than you ever have before.

The kind of relaxation I am talking about begins with clearing your mind of your preprogrammed beliefs, melting away stress, and patiently dismissing the constant internal chatter that disrupts your focus. Most people do not know how to relax in this way. It is a skill perfected by those who truly understand the power of the mind and how it can work for you.

Mastering these relaxation techniques and practicing them daily will give you access to the deepest levels of your mind, while also promoting personal accountability toward self-improvement and self-discovery. Relaxing is the first step toward eliminating doubt and the fear of failure from your mental processes. It will allow you to become the commander in chief of your own life so that you can set terms and achieve goals to drive your own success.

Did you know that relaxing is a daily habit of many successful people? When you discover the benefits of relaxation, it's easy to understand why: relaxing reduces stress, boosts productivity, increases focus and concentration, reduces depression, and can improve physical and mental health overall.

Intentional relaxation allows us to take advantage of our brain's neuroplasticity, which is the ability to use our experiences and perceptions to restructure the brain and better our lives.

That is why relaxing is the first step in this 14-day program. This is the beginning of a continual growth process, and you will begin to see the results immediately...but only by committing to this program.

Relaxation is interpreted several ways by different individuals. For some, running a triathlon is relaxing. For others, relaxation means kicking back in a recliner and reading a book. But for our intent and purpose, relaxation is a much more deliberate undertaking. It is not one half of R&R—"rest and relaxation." It is so critical to well-being that it deserves to stand on its own, apart from "rest." Relaxation is 100 percent physical and 100 percent mental.

"Relaxation is 100 percent physical and 100 percent mental.

When we stop activity, we relax our muscles. Our minds, however, are still in work mode. It is a common misconception that entertainment, or any other activity that does not require physical exertion, is relaxation. It might be relaxing to the muscles, but it will not necessarily relax the mind. Because of that misconception, many people do not know how to truly relax. People tell us to relax, we tell ourselves to relax, and we may think we are doing just that; however, our mind is not 100 percent reacting to that command.

In our society, there is an immense amount of pressure to do well at work, school, activities, and sports. As a result, we're often running at full throttle around the clock, never pausing to reflect and recharge. It is difficult for most individuals to find a few minutes each day to relax their mind. Common excuses are: "I don't have time to relax; there is too much to do" or "This is too important—I will relax when I am done." We are all guilty of this, and because the world in which we live becomes more of a pressure cooker each year, it is vital to our health and well-being that we learn how to relax and make it a daily priority.

From this moment forward, you will begin to carve out "me time" during your day. This time will become your intentional relaxation period. You will expose your conscious and subconscious mind to new paths to relaxation and decompression.

Today, I will share three simple strategies that you can use to create and reinforce the habit of relaxation. It is vital that you use them to take action and make relaxation a part of your daily life. Just like healthy eating is a lifestyle, relaxation is a lifestyle, and you must learn to view it that way. Your relaxation routine should become automatic, like brushing your teeth in the morning or showering. With that in mind, consider these three simple, yet incredibly effective forms of relaxation. In order to relax, you need to ACT:

> **AIR—INTENTIONAL BREATHING**

> **CHANGE YOUR IMAGERY**

> **TAKE TIME TO RECHARGE**

AIR—INTENTIONAL BREATHING

Breathing is an involuntary movement. Breathing for relaxation, however, is intentional. It takes thought and control to deliberately inhale and exhale and to be fully aware of the impact this process has both physically and mentally on our bodies.

Please try this exercise right now. Slowly and deeply breathe in. Listen to the air as it enters your body. Feel it as it moves through you, entering your lungs. Feel your lungs expand to capacity, and then hold your breath for a moment. Next, breathe out. Exhale, slowly releasing the cleansing air. Feel your lungs as they slowly deflate, and feel the air as it leaves your body.

Did you notice how this simple act of breathing cleansed your body and mind? Did you notice how just one slow breath left you feeling more relaxed, focused, and grounded? Imagine how these benefits can and will increase with each additional slow, deliberate breath you take.

It is worth noticing that the process of breathing has two dimensions. In the first dimension, breathing is a life function that keeps oxygen flowing through our lungs and into our bloodstream. It is an involuntary movement.

The second dimension is conscious breathing, which has the power to eliminate stress, while also increasing our focus and concentration. Conscious breathing is a powerful tool that is constantly at our disposal and can be utilized any time we want. This technique has been used in meditation and yoga for centuries to cleanse the body and the soul. It is a form of relaxation that is taught in classes to help women through childbirth. It can be a natural sedative. It is also a stimulant, providing us with the energy and life source needed for survival.

Dedicating a few minutes every day specifically to breathing is essential to our well-being. Bringing awareness to the forefront of your mind can and will produce remarkable benefits in your daily life. You will find yourself less stressed and better equipped to face challenges and obstacles in every minute of your day. Your thought processes and concentration will be more focused, enabling you to be more aware and more present in every aspect of your life.

It is amazing that one of the best relaxation techniques is something you have done your whole life—breathe. It's incredible that something so basic and natural can become your simplest method of de-stressing. It is so important for you to carve out time each day to breathe. By doing so in a controlled and intentional manner, you will be on your way to a new you! You will be someone who is more focused and relaxed, ready to take on life. After all, isn't that what we all truly desire? Let me help you achieve this. I will be with you every step of the way.

CHANGE YOUR IMAGERY

The environment in which we place ourselves can have a profound impact on our mind. Consider, for instance, the reality that most people do not enjoy going to a physician. It has been proven that some people have higher blood pressure when they are at the doctor's office. This is so commonplace that it even has a name—white coat syndrome. For most of us, there are additional situations and environments that can create similar reactions.

Are you aware that even if you do not like where you are physically or figuratively, you can change your mental outlook and turn it into a positive experience? The greatest gift we have been given is the ability to control our thought processes. Yes, you are always in the driver's seat and have the ability to choose the path that is best for you. Relaxation techniques play a vital role in cultivating this mindset.

Relaxation can be achieved by directing your mind to a calm and de-stressed state of being. Mental images can take you to a relaxed and peaceful place in your mind. Guided imagery, or the recreation of sensory experiences and the stimulation of mental content through evoked mental images, is a powerful technique whose impact we will discuss later in this book. For the purposes of relaxation, this approach can take you from where you are to a place that is more enjoyable.

Challenging experiences happen to all of us. They are a part of life. Negative thoughts do not discriminate. It does not matter if you are the CEO of a company or a parent worrying about a child—negativity has a way of creeping into our thoughts and compromising our mental and physical well-being. Being in a difficult position is not an enjoyable place, but how we choose to face these frustrations is entirely up to us. Let me guide you to a place of constant focus and positive reinforcement so that when trying situations occur, you know how to control your thoughts and bring about change.

The next time you feel stress and tension, remove yourself from that thought or location. Find a quiet environment and envision a relaxing place that brings you joy. Fully experience it. If your relaxing place is a park, picture the bright blue sky. Feel the gentle breeze against your skin. Smell the clean scent of freshly cut grass while you are listening to the sounds of nature around you. Relax against these sights and sounds until you feel yourself becoming calmer and more peaceful. Find your calming space and enter it without inhibitions. Let yourself go, breathe, and relax.

This state of relaxation can be achieved by anyone. You just have to take the time to breathe in and relax and think about what calms you. What is your tranquil mindset? Where is your happy place? Close your eyes and find that peaceful place and go there. Where you go does not matter as long as you choose an undisturbed, quiet environment that makes you feel relaxed. The point is to change the channel in your mind and visualize a safe, serene place where you can relax for a few minutes.

By combining guided imagery with relaxation, you will improve your cognitive abilities and focus. Other benefits include better memory, the ability to learn new skills faster, and enhanced visualization skills, which improve right-brain thinking. Relaxation through guided imagery also strengthens the connection between the left and right hemisphere of the brain, and it deepens the connection to your subconscious.

TAKE TIME TO RECHARGE

After you finish reading this chapter, please take a few minutes and listen to "Day Two" in the audio program. This is a short track, and the length is intentional because I want to show you that you can relax and reap the results regardless of how busy you are. How can you not have a few minutes in a day to spend on something that will greatly benefit you? The relaxation exercise in this audio track is designed to help you relax, and you can do this simply by listening to my voice! It requires no special preparation. It contains no hypnotic suggestions. It is intended for one purpose—to help you achieve a relaxed, calm state of mind.

Simple, right? Find a quiet place where you can sit comfortably for just a few minutes. Close the door, and escape the everyday stresses and distractions of life. Just hit "play," and listen to my voice. Follow me. Give me a few minutes of your full attention, and I will help you to relax. I want you to become part of an elite group of individuals who have harnessed my relaxation techniques for over three-plus decades to lead less stressful, more fulfilling lives—while boosting their performance at the same time.

ESTABLISH A DAILY ROUTINE AND ACT

ACT! Air and Intentional Breathing, Change Your Imagery, and Take Time to Recharge. Using these three simple techniques, you can invite relaxation into your world on a daily basis. They can be performed at any time and any place without difficulty. I would like you to commit to doing all three every day. ACT! Can you do that?

Once again, let me emphasize that relaxation is most effective when it is a part of your daily routine. We all know the old saying "you are what you eat"—well, it is just as important to remember that you are also what you think. When your mind is full of stress, you become tense and worried. You cannot concentrate or focus. You are less productive and have a poor outlook. However, when you make relaxation a part of your daily life, you have a better outlook and fewer worries.

"You are what you think.

Take just a few minutes to relax every day using these three simple strategies and watch how relaxation will carry over into everything you do. I guarantee that you will be glad you did.

SOFTWARE UPDATES

> Creating "me time" is vital in every area of your life. Give yourself permission to invest in yourself, your growth, and your success.

> The simple act of conscious, deliberate breathing will clear your mind, providing greater focus and clarity, and it is a free and very effective stress reducer that has incredibly positive side effects.

> Guided imagery will help you relax by transferring you from stressful situations and surroundings into a calm and peaceful environment.

PROGRESSIVE JUMPS

> Stop everything for a few minutes and relax. Breathe intentionally and allow the air to relax you as it enters your body.

> Change your imagery. Use your mind to take yourself to a place or time when you were happy or successful. Relive the moment and remove yourself from anxiety and stress.

> Now, take the time to recharge. Listen to "Day Two" in the audio support program. Notice how you become more relaxed and reinvigorated.

LANGUAGE

"Words are magic to receptive listeners, as well
as to the person who speaks them."

AS YOU'VE DISCOVERED in previous chapters, there are two types of AutoThoughts—constructive and destructive. Everything that follows in Days 3 through 14 will be about helping you to maximize constructive thoughts…and minimize destructive thoughts.

I have already given you one extremely powerful tool for leaning into those constructive AutoThoughts and disentangling yourself from the destructive ones: relaxation. If you have done all three of the daily relaxation activities we discussed, congratulations! You are on the right track. If you have not yet completed all three relaxation activities, please make sure you do them before you go any further.

Planting constructive thoughts in your subconscious mind so that you can benefit from them when you need them is nothing more or less than mastering the art of self-suggestion while your mind is clear and calm. This is when we are the most receptive to our thoughts. That is why getting into the habit of relaxing on a regular basis—and not just during times of high stress or difficulty—is so important. If you do the work of programming your mindset when you're at peak receptivity, you will not only function at a higher level overall, but you will be able to leverage the power of these amplified thoughts when you are faced with both opportunities and challenges. Don't forget—you can manufacture this receptivity even when your mental resources are drained or under duress by harnessing the power of relaxation.

Now that you have begun to install the habit of relaxation, the question becomes: What do you do while you are there?

One powerful answer to that question is: leverage the awesome, but usually neglected, power of language. Words are just letters…until you give them meaning! Then they become forces for transformation.

Language—the words we choose to say, think, and reinforce—are humankind's great underutilized tool when it comes to constructive self-suggestion. But here's the irony: we're *already* masters of language for self-suggestion. We just don't always realize that we're good at it, and as a result, we might not always harness the immense power of words in the most constructive way. Too often, we focus on and feed our destructive thoughts. We water the weeds, making them grow stronger.

Here's an example of a destructive AutoThought that we may have been unconsciously enforcing on a regular basis: "I hate driving in traffic" or "This traffic is terrible." That's a message a lot of us choose to send to ourselves over and over again. We use words to create the reality that we hate traffic, that it's terrible. Every day, we use language to persuade ourselves to think like this on a deep, unconscious level. As a result, not only do we not like traffic, but that dislike grows over time and we feel it without even thinking about it.

This has been happening since we were children. Think about the countless kids who have never tasted broccoli (or whatever food it is their parents want them to eat) but still insist they hate it. Why do they do that? It is because they've leveraged the power of language to persuade themselves to believe that they really do hate broccoli. They've given themselves the verbal and mental suggestion that broccoli isn't good and there's no way they'll ever like it: "I HATE BROCCOLI!" Guess what? They really do! They've convinced themselves of it by repeating the idea to themselves until their thoughts became their reality. Guess what else? We are all that kid! We have just replaced broccoli with traffic!

We are all prone to using language to send ourselves disempowering, destructive messages like "I HATE (FILL IN THE BLANK)!" Oftentimes that habit does not serve us well. For one thing, those types of messages focus on something negative— namely, the powerful negative emotions of hatred and dislike, which inhibit our mental processes and have very real somatic consequences. For another, it keeps us from experiencing something we might actually enjoy. When we use the power of language to focus on what we do not like, do not want, do not have, and so on, we are needlessly limiting ourselves.

Most of us have plenty of personal experience with this. The good news is, we can always make positive conscious choices about the words we use to frame our experience.

WORDS MATTER

The words we think, say, and reinforce during the course of our day really do matter. They can be an incredibly powerful motivator for our emotions and our actions. They can captivate us, command our attention, inspire us, compel us to buy products, help us form new relationships, and alter our performance. On a larger scale, the words we use have the power to completely transform who we are as well as the lens through which we view the world.

However, negative, destructive words can limit us significantly. They can cause us to be consumed with fear and worry. They can paralyze us and convince us that we are not capable or qualified. They can cement the belief that we will fail at something before we even try. Destructive language gives us preconceived notions and preordained outcomes that discourage us from pursuing goals, making it seem like our dreams are impossible to achieve.

All too often, though, we fall into familiar but destructive habits when it comes to language...by replaying what I call "broccoli messages." (For instance: "I hate driving in traffic," when traffic can actually be an opportunity to do things like listen to motivational audiobooks that inspire us.) We may even abandon our immense power to choose language that empowers and motivates us and give that power to somebody else! If you've ever found yourself repeating the words of a catchy commercial jingle—and I bet you have—then you know exactly what I'm talking about.

Today is all about developing purposeful, constructive language that you can use both inside and outside a state of relaxation. Let me define that for you. Constructive language is the selection and combination of specific words to convey a specific, intentional thought to produce a desired result, action, or emotion.

Leveraging constructive language is an extremely important aspect of the AutoThoughts process. The conscious use of language creates awareness of and attention to the words we use when we think and speak…awareness that can broaden our scope of communication with ourselves and others.

The words we use, especially when we talk to our ourselves, can plant belief or doubt, motivation or discouragement, fear or excitement, and anxiety or peace. *You really can* choose your words wisely, reinforcing the best ones so that you can choose your dominant emotions, results, and actions. *You really can* use language to create momentum toward your dreams, desires, and goals. With just a little practice, you will find that leveraging constructive language becomes a powerful daily awakening for you—an awakening that can open the door to unlimited possibilities. With consistency and commitment, you will rewrite the software that runs your mindset, replacing destructive thoughts and beliefs with constructive ones. The great news is that this will become a habit, and you will eventually be able to do it without thinking about it at all.

What follows are details about select insights related to language that have been very helpful for me and countless clients over the years. These insights relate to trigger words and reframing.

TRIGGER WORDS

Certain words are powerful because they have the potential to trigger our attention and point our resulting emotions and actions in a certain direction. It's worth considering such words very closely.

Think about a word like *now*. When someone asks us to do something, we listen, but we may postpone making a decision about whether we'll actually do it. Yet when they ask us to do something *now*, we are more likely to say "yes" or "no" to their request immediately. There is an urgency to words like "now" that communicates a sense of importance and compels us to respond with the same urgency.

There is another powerful trigger word I'd like you to build into your arsenal. Let me ask you this: What is the single most powerful word someone can say to you? What, for that matter, is the most powerful word you can say to someone else? Without a doubt, the most persuasive, hypnotic word in everybody's life is the one word we all consider to be just as unique as we are: our own name.

This makes perfect sense. From the time we were babies, our name quickly became the biggest attention-grabbing word we would ever hear. Every time we hear it, we know someone is speaking directly to us and that whatever they have to say is meant for us and us alone. When your parents called you by name, you listened. When teachers caught you daydreaming, they said your name and you snapped into attention. When you get mail with your name on it, you are instantly persuaded to open the envelope and read it. When the phone rings and someone asks for you by name, you take the call. When you are in a public place and hear someone call out your name, you stop in your tracks and look all around with deep focus and attention—and then maybe feel a little awkward when you realize they were calling someone else.

Whenever we hear our own name, we automatically listen more closely, assume some degree of accountability and responsibility for paying attention, and understand that something is being told specifically to us. That is a very powerful piece of language! Our name is the one thing that follows us throughout our life. It is a part of our identity and, therefore, one of the most important trigger words we can leverage.

Our name is such an integral part of our identity that even when we are not in a conscious state, we respond to it. Scientific evidence published in the *Journal of Neurology, Neurosurgery, and Psychiatry* shows that people in a persistent vegetative state (PVS) have brain activity in response to language, even though they don't respond to other stimuli and give no indication that they are aware of their environment. Brain imaging showed reliably higher brain activity when researchers spoke the unconscious patients' names out loud, with noticeably lower brain activity when other, random names were spoken.[3]

Constructive self-messaging using your own name is something you can take advantage of in a powerful way at any moment. I often send myself audible messages like, "Come on, Ricky. You know you can do this." By using my own name, I am telling myself to pay attention, because I'm giving myself an important suggestion.

Words that signify our names are almost as powerful. The first word that comes to mind is the pronoun "I." When we use this pronoun in a constructive way, i.e., to send ourselves a positive message, we can quickly lay the foundation for powerful emotions and actions. For some people, this pronoun is an even more effective trigger than their own name!

Words like *think* and *envision* are also great trigger words because they open unlimited possibilities. Whenever someone asks us to *think*, that request launches our thought processes. Yes, we already were thinking, but giving the active suggestion encourages a deeper level of conscious thinking. Once we actively engage our brain, anything is possible. *Envision* is just as powerful because it signifies that something that is not a part of our current reality could be, as a result of our personal choice to make it visible. Again, the possibilities are endless.

Words that promote the creative use of our minds are extremely powerful triggers. These are just a few that have worked for me. You may find others that work for you.

So let's say you are facing some kind of challenge. Build a moment into your day where you close your eyes and say out loud, "Now I am envisioning a positive outcome." Give yourself one full minute (or more) to envision that outcome. What do you see?

USING WORDS TO REFRAME YOUR SITUATION

We all talk to ourselves, whether silently or out loud, whether we realize that's what we're doing or not. That's just how human beings are wired. The words we use when we talk to ourselves create a mindset that can be either positive or negative.

Consciously chosen words can help us gain a new perspective on any situation, even if it initially seems negative to us. Learning to use language to reframe our reality constructively as the day unfolds is a powerful skill, one that you can master. Here are two powerful examples of how you can begin.

Change "but" to "and." A simple word like *but* can often produce unintended negative resonances inside your head. When we hear "but," we know that a contradiction to what was previously said is on its way, and we immediately move into a skeptical, unproductive state of mind. Our mind automatically listens for the upcoming contradiction. Here is an example: "This software package is the solution to all of your company's HR needs, *but* it will typically take about 30 days to install and learn how to use."

That sounds pretty negative, doesn't it? What would happen if one word was changed in that sentence, and that one word suggested that 30 days wasn't a disadvantage, but an advantage? Changing the word *but* to *and* transforms the meaning by reframing the entire experience: "This software package is the solution to all of your company's HR needs, *and* it will typically take only about 30 days to install and learn how to use."

Suddenly, we are suggesting to the listener that 30 days is a small investment. There is nothing deceptive here; we are still communicating the same message, but now we are portraying the 30 days in a positive manner. We are reframing the experience and how we perceive the outcome.

You can do the same with messages you send to yourself. "I am earning a good living...*but* I could be earning a lot more if I added three more commissions every quarter." Compare that to "I am earning a good salary...*and* I could be earning even more if I added three more commissions every quarter."

Another favorite reframing strategy I use, and coach my clients to use, is replacing "I'll try" with "I will." "I will" instills confidence and determination, while "I'll try" is an admittance that what you're trying to do might not be possible. "I will" is an internal promise that you will, while "I'll try" puts the thought in your mind that it might not happen. This provides a ready-made excuse when you're not successful and often produces a lackluster effort.

Other negative words that can send your brain unsupportive messages include *not, impossible,* and *can't.* How often do we give ourselves excuses, telling ourselves—erroneously—why something can't be done? Example: "It is impossible for me to meet this deadline." You can learn to edit these words out, too, and instantly reframe both the thought and the situation. As in: "I am getting closer to completing this project on time."

How many doors would we unlock, how many creative solutions could we find, if we opened our mind to possibilities, instead of limiting them by using negative, destructive self-talk?

WHO ARE YOU, REALLY?

I had the most interesting experience a while back. I was on an airplane flight, and I happened to strike up a conversation with the gentleman sitting next to me. I'll call him Mark. I asked Mark, "What do you do?"

This is a pretty common question, of course, and I have asked it thousands of times while interacting with new acquaintances. Maybe you have, too. But Mark's response floored me. Here is what he said:

"Ricky," he said, "I help individuals and corporations with critical services that are vital to annual challenges and procedures. I am the guy my clients rely on year after year!"

Now, normally, when I ask someone, "What do you do?" I hear something not very exciting in response: "I'm in marketing." "I'm a systems analyst." "I'm a salesperson." Sometimes there is even a hint of regret or dissatisfaction in the person's voice, body language, and facial expression, as though they are actually apologizing for their life's calling. Not Mark! He made a conscious decision to use language to convey his deep passion for what he did. In doing so, he told me who he really was! Yes, Mark is an accountant.

Imagine if Mark was asked that question in a job interview, and he answered it just like he did with me. Now imagine another candidate being asked the same question, but he answers it with, "I'm an accountant based in Atlanta." Who do you think would get the job?

As we close this chapter, I challenge you to do exactly what Mark did. Come up with your own answer to the question "What do you do?" Spend some time on this. Create two or three sentences that concisely convey your great passion in life—the reason you're here on earth. Take a couple of passes at this. Write your answer down. Then say it out loud, and start sharing it with other people. As you answer that question "What do you do?" in an utterly unique way, be sure the words you choose connect to the deeper, unspoken question that always lies within that common conversational query: "Who are you?" Mark assumed that was what I was really asking...so his words pointed toward his true passion in life!

The language you choose to leverage in response to the question "Who are you?" will deliver the perfect answer to that critical question of what you do...for others and for you. Find those words!

Your language creates your reality. Use it wisely!

SOFTWARE UPDATES

> Language is a powerful, but underutilized, tool that anyone can use. We already use our thoughts and self-suggestion in creating our perspective, attitudes, and, therefore, our reality. Discover how positive language can develop constructive thinking on a habitual basis.

> Trigger words can motivate, change expectations, or create a sense of urgency. What trigger words do you use? What words can you substitute them with to create a different, more empowering reality?

> You can reframe any situation simply by thinking of it differently. Changing one word in a thought can totally transform your outlook.

PROGRESSIVE JUMPS

> Create and practice your passionate answer to the question "What do you do?" Start sharing it with other people.

> Consciously begin to notice the words you use, and make a deliberate effort to reframe your sentences in a constructive way, changing "but" to "and," "I'll try" to "I will," and "I can't" to "I can."

> Use people's names when speaking to them, and notice how they respond.

> As a reinforcement tool, you can now listen to "Day Three" in the audio support program.

GRATITUDE

"You have the ability to positively affect the attitude of everyone around you—including yourself—by choosing to build gratitude into your daily life."

GRATITUDE IS A PRACTICAL STRATEGY for inviting more positive things into your life. By using language to change your emotional outlook from one of stress and disappointment to one of gratitude, you can transform your state of mind...and your entire experience of living.

The wisest people have taught this for thousands of years. Gratitude works, and there is scientific research to prove it. A study conducted at UC Berkeley found that fMRI scans of people who expressed gratitude for three months showed distinct brain activity. In addition, they had higher neural sensitivity in the medial prefrontal cortex, which is the area of the brain responsible for decision-making and learning.[4]

This study doesn't stand alone. There is no shortage of research that touts the benefits of expressing gratitude. We know it works... but why does it work?

Every word, thought, suggestion, and experience that you invite into your subconscious mind molds your reality. Your subconscious mind, or mindset, has a powerful influence over your actions, reactions, emotions, attitude, and outcomes. It's like a fire that you can keep burning with different kinds of fuel: clean and sweet-smelling, or smoky and foul.

The fuel you use to feed your fire is the single most important factor in creating the life and reality you want. When you choose gratitude to keep the fire burning, you choose the best fuel of all.

One of my favorite stories about gratitude involves the legendary inventor and entrepreneur Thomas Edison. Faced with what most of us would consider an unspeakable tragedy, Edison found a way to turn misfortune into something for which he could be grateful. When he learned that his factory had burned to the ground, the great inventor smiled and said, "All our mistakes are burned up. Thank God we can start anew."

Notice what happened there. Edison realized he had the right to decide what this seemingly unfortunate experience meant. He exercised that right and chose to view his situation as something for which he could be thankful. This is a perfect example showing the gratitude muscle Edison built up, one that anyone can develop—you included. We all have the ability to grow and use our gratitude muscle.

Edison had plenty of practice in fueling himself and his sub-conscious mind with this attitude of gratitude. As a direct result of that practice, he built a positive platform on which he could live his life, no matter what took place. He had an unshakeable belief that there was always something to be grateful for, even in times of misfortune. This mindset enabled Edison to maximize his creative capacity, identify opportunities in times of adversity, and innovate in important, dynamic ways.

MAKE A CONSCIOUS CHOICE

Today, you will gain the understanding that you have the sole power and absolute control over your reality, and you can make it a grateful one. Today, you decide that you can and will build up your own gratitude muscle. Today, you begin creating a clear space for gratitude in your life. You begin believing in and acting on the transformative power of gratitude. You begin making conscious choices that make gratitude your natural response.

How will this impact your life? Gratitude pulls us out of self-pity, worry, and anxiety. As a result, we create awareness from the opportunities that are available to us. The subconscious records everything we see and focus on and directs energy toward that goal. When we focus on the negative, our thoughts—and, there-fore, emotions and actions—will also focus on the negative. How-ever, when the focus is on gratitude, which is powerfully positive, our mindset will also focus our thoughts, emotions, and actions toward more of the same.

You can update your mindset to focus on gratitude. Making a conscious choice to view a potentially stressful event from a different perspective and then repeating that choice as the day moves forward is the key to making gratitude a reality in your life. This is a total transformation of perception.

Language plays a huge role in this transformation. For instance, instead of saying, "I've got to go to work," try "I get to go to work." Notice how a tiny change like that can bring about a totally different attitude, along with a whole new set of questions about the experience: "What can I learn at work today? How can I improve? How can I become more fulfilled today?" Those are gratitude-focused questions. And they originate from the language you choose to feed your mindset.

So instead of worrying about things you do not have, might lose, or are unhappy with, you can use language—both spoken and unspoken—to create gratitude for what you already possess. Gratitude is the most powerful way to invite more positive things into your life. By transitioning your outlook regarding any experience from a negative position to a position of gratitude, you also change your state of mind.

Stress reduction is a component of this program and one I teach to my audiences. Do you know what the number one stress reliever is? Gratitude. Yes, it's as simple as that. This feeling of gratitude is important, because when stress levels are lowered, your quality of life, health, and happiness will improve.

Problems and obstacles will always exist in life. Being late for work and getting stopped by every red light along the way is an experience to which everyone can relate. It's the perspective and attitude we use in dealing with our "red lights" that determine our outcomes. For some, these inconveniences, or red lights, carry too much weight. They are given too much attention and become obstacles standing in the way of our mental success. Through our own thoughts and suggestions, we can remind ourselves that the current problem is a minor inconvenience when looking at the big picture. We can even see a major challenge as an opportunity to make a change, one that will drive growth and fulfillment. This is what helped me deal with the sadness of my friend Mike's cancer diagnosis: I found a way to use what happened to him to gain perspective and create positive meaning in my life.

We can always use a reminder that our obstacles aren't huge hurdles that we cannot conquer. Rather, they are only small bumps in the path that can easily be surmounted so that we can achieve a positive mindset. Once we have given ourselves that reminder, we can begin to reshape our reality, changing it from unfortunate to fortunate and from a state of victimhood to one of empowerment.

There is always something to be grateful for every day, every hour, every minute. The following is a great example. A woman was diagnosed with breast cancer, and while recovering from a double mastectomy, she found it more comfortable to sleep in a recliner in her living room. While she was asleep one night, flames triggered her alarm system, which woke her up in time to escape her house. Here is a woman with a terminal diagnosis and she has just lost her home. She chose in that moment to take a step back and look at the big picture: she was grateful she had undergone surgery that forced her to sleep in the living room, where she had an easy exit during the fire.

We don't have to experience negative events like this to find reasons to be grateful. You also do not need to spend hours thinking of what you are grateful for. It can be something as simple as being grateful for every breath you take. Appreciate that breath of air as you inhale, focus your awareness on it, exhale, and then repeat the process. When we are grateful for the positive things in our life, we attract more of them. When we dwell on the negative, we invite more trouble and stress into our life. Conscious gratitude is the secret ingredient that makes true success and true happiness possible. The more we practice it, the more happiness and success we are able to attract.

"When we are grateful for the positive things in our life, we attract more of them.

When you create awareness of what you are grateful for in your thoughts and your mental programming, you begin to associate different thoughts and suggestions with your day-to-day experiences. Consciously reminding yourself to identify something to be thankful for in every experience will create a new, positive habit, and your habitual response of gratitude will become automatic.

Start putting your mindset to work. Exercise your gratitude muscle regularly. Plant different suggestions of appreciation in your mind, where it can produce the harvest of an enhanced outlook, a broader perspective, and the ability to thrive during challenging times. Get rid of the negativity, and focus with conscious intent on what is positive, what is working, and what you are grateful for—and you'll begin to see more positive, more generative results.

FROM STRESS TO GRATITUDE

Right now, I want you to think of an experience you encounter regularly, on a daily basis, that typically makes you feel stressed. For many people, driving to or from work is such a stressful experience. For others, it could be getting the kids out the door on time in the morning.

When we encounter that stressful experience every day, it is very easy to make a mental list of all the things we aren't grateful for and would like to avoid. Maybe you've already started making such a list in your head, thinking you would rather be doing anything other than dealing with rush-hour traffic. If so, I challenge you to make a different mental list and find something you can *choose* to be grateful for in that experience. Yes, gratitude is a choice, and it must be a deliberate, conscious effort before it can become a habit.

When I ask people to find something to be grateful for in their stressful situations, their force-of-habit response is usually something like, "I can't." Or I often hear, "If you gave me a week, I might be able to think of something." Or even: "Maybe I could be grateful for something else."

Seriously?

Maybe you can be grateful for the opportunity to have some alone time to listen to music, audiobooks, or podcast programs that can re-energize you. Maybe you can be grateful that you have a job to drive to…and reliable transportation. You can be grateful that the driver who cut you off didn't cause an accident. You can be grateful that this situation and experience is temporary and you know you will eventually get to your destination. Be grateful that you're going to get there safely and *only* be ten minutes late.

Right now, you can make a mental list of all the positive things to which that habitually stressful event connects in your life. And you know what? You're going to.

Think of at least seven things that are positive, or could be positive, about this daily event. For instance, if what stresses you out is driving to work in the morning, you might create this list:

> ❭ I have a car to drive. There are people who don't.

> ❭ I have a place to live, from which I can leave to go to work. There are many homeless individuals who do not have shelter or food.

> ❭ I live in a city that provides me with access to everything I need when I need it. Many people live in rural areas without the conveniences afforded by city living.

> When I drive, I can choose to turn the phone and radio off and enjoy silent time to myself, which is valuable time for me to relax and recharge my system.

> Alternatively, I can choose to listen to music, podcasts, or audiobooks as I drive, which is also enjoyable.

> I am employed. My job, career, and responsibilities have meaning, bringing me purpose and fulfillment.

> I appreciate my friendships, colleagues, and relationships.

> I can look forward to the experience of returning home and spending time with the person or people I love.

Take this opportunity, right now, to identify at least seven things about that habitually stressful experience for which you could be grateful. It's not hard once you get the hang of it. As you assemble your mental list, remember how powerful it is to be able to learn from an experience and how that in and of itself is another thing to appreciate.

You can always find something for which you can be grateful. You always have the power to determine what an experience means. You can always choose to make an experience mean something that points your life toward gratitude.

SOFTWARE UPDATES

> Gratitude creates distinct brain activity and can improve decision-making and learning.

> You have a choice as to how you interpret any situation in your life. The choice you make will have a significant impact on your awareness, attitude, and opportunities.

> The practice of gratitude is an effective way to prevent and reduce stress. It is free and can attract an abundance of the things you want in life, so remember to always focus on what you want!

PROGRESSIVE JUMPS

> Write down the seven things you discovered that you are grateful for.

> As you make your way through the day, identify at least seven more things you could be grateful for. Write those down, too. Get into the habit of exercising your gratitude muscle. Use gratitude to shift your focus from what you imagine your life lacks to the abundance that is already waiting for you.

> Consider keeping a gratitude journal every day, and challenge yourself to expand the things you are grateful

for over time. I find it very easy to use my Notes app on my phone to create a "Gratitude List." That way, it is easy to access, and it is always with me.

> As a reinforcement tool, you can now listen to "Day Four" in the audio support program.

COMMITMENT

"Don't invest your emotions and thoughts into
things you don't like—invest in the
things you appreciate most."

WHEN YOU SEE a professional whose time is expensive, someone who makes you book the appointment in advance, do you typically show up on time?

I am talking about an accountant, an attorney, a therapist, a doctor—that kind of professional. Do you make a habit of being late to these meetings, or do you make a habit of showing up on time...or maybe even slightly early?

When I ask this question, most people acknowledge that they make a point of showing up just a little bit early for such appointments. They put reminders in their calendars. They leave themselves sticky notes on their desk. They make arrangements to take the necessary time off from work. They leave themselves plenty of time to get from point A to point B, find a parking space, and so on. They do what's necessary.

In a word, they are committed.

You probably are, too. When you pay for someone's time, you arrive at least a few minutes early. You want to make the most of the time that's been set aside for you.

You are committed. But you're also limited. You are limited to the time that the professional has set aside on their calendar for you. It is a short window of time, and you want to make the most of every minute of it, so you arrive early. You give them all the power and authority. Why? Because you are paying for their time and you know their time is valuable. You want to be sure you get everything you possibly can out of that private session.

WHAT ABOUT YOU?

Here's another question: Since we know that you are your most important asset, doesn't it make sense to schedule a little time with yourself each day? And shouldn't you give that time the same level of commitment you would if you were booking time with an accountant, attorney, or doctor? Wouldn't you want to get every-thing you possibly could from your most precious asset…and be deeply committed to it?

We all have good intentions, but a lack of commitment has an impact on our outcomes. Here's proof: *U.S. News & World Report* states that New Year's resolutions have an 80 percent failure rate. Need more? More than 90 percent of new businesses fail within the first two years, and one of the underlying reasons is a lack of commitment.

So doesn't it make sense that if you want to achieve growth or success in any area of your life, you should give it the same level of commitment that you give to the time you schedule with others? What if you acknowledged to yourself that *your* time really is the most valuable time of all?

With that idea in mind, today you begin creating, and scheduling, a private session for yourself…with yourself. This is a truly powerful success habit.

Schedule time with yourself every day. Block that time out in your planner so that you are reminded to give it the same level of commitment that you would for other appointments. Arrive on time, or maybe a few minutes early. Then clear your mind of everything else so that you can focus on this appointment and nothing else. Remember, your time is the most valuable of all, so you don't want any distractions.

The beauty of this habit is that it puts you in complete control. You have the power and the authority. You're not hustling to match up with somebody else's time window. No. You are committed…*to yourself.* And you keep that commitment.

Sometimes people push back a little when I tell them that this success habit is a non-negotiable part of Leverage Your Mindset. They come up with all kinds of reasons not to schedule just a little bit of time with themselves each day. They tell me that they are not "schedule people" and prefer to improvise. Some say that they work better when under pressure. Others claim that they have too many other things on their calendar and just don't have 5, 10, or 15 consecutive minutes a day for themselves.

If any of those thoughts crossed your mind, press "pause" for a moment and reconsider.

You *are* a "schedule person"—when you decide to be. If you weren't a schedule person, you wouldn't go to work on time every day. If you weren't a schedule person, you would never file your taxes, visit the doctor, or pick up your kids from school. If you've ever done any of those things, you probably left yourself a reminder—a note on the refrigerator, an entry on a physical calendar, or a simple alarm on your phone—that told you when you had to take an important action…before it was too late. It was all part of your commitment to keeping your appointments and promises. Well, that is exactly what you're going to be doing here. The only difference is you are doing it for you, not for the doctor, the IRS, or your kids.

Yes, you might prefer to improvise, and you might work better under pressure. There is no shame in that. But know that you can still improvise around your scheduled appointments. It's also true that you will work better under pressure when you start formally scheduling some "you time" each and every day. That is a promise.

As for the "I'm too busy" response, do yourself a favor and acknowledge right now that this is an excuse…and not a particularly convincing one. Are you really so busy that you don't have time to invest five or ten minutes a day into yourself? I guarantee you that you can find five or ten minutes during even the busiest of days. How much time do you spend surfing the Internet? On social media? Watching television? I rest my case.

Once you have set aside a few minutes a day to yourself, what will you do with that time? This is the time when you will focus entirely on you. It is your time to breathe deeply, remove all distractions, and relax. It is when you gain the greatest access to your mindset, so it is the perfect time to focus on constructive thoughts that will remove self-doubt and replace it with belief. The time you spend entirely with yourself is one of self-discovery and awareness, where you can visualize and affirm the goals, growth, and success you desire. Commit to investing this time into the things you want and that matter the most to you.

This is your moment of truth. This is the point at which you either begin to really benefit from what we're exploring together in this program…or you set what we're doing aside and choose not to learn, grow, and benefit from what you're getting here. *If you don't create some daily commitment around what we're doing together, nothing I'm going to share with you on subsequent days will do you any good. That's the reality.*

SCHEDULE IT NOW

Here is my challenge to you: Schedule it now! Right now. Pull out your calendar and schedule the time. Start today. Take the time you are spending right now, reading this chapter, and enter it into your daily schedule. This is your daily "you time." It is your commitment to yourself.

For now, you will spend this time implementing this program. Formalize that time. Put it in your calendar. Gradually increase the increments of time you block off on your schedule. Set an alarm for the calendar reminder and hold yourself accountable.

Now that you've made that formal commitment and scheduled it, I assume that means *you are now following through on your commitment to spend some scheduled "you time" with yourself.* You have booked this appointment with yourself, and you are now totally committed to getting the very most out of this session.

Congratulations!

During the rest of the time scheduled for this session, we are going to practice picking up the mental remote control and pointing it toward a channel of your choosing.

CHANGE THE CHANNEL

You always have access to the remote control. You always have the power to change the channel; to free your mind; to be more motivated, more successful, and more driven toward a positive outcome. You always can change your thought process from doubt, disbelief, or frustration to gratitude. Let me give you an example of this right now.

Make sure you are in a quiet place where you won't be disturbed. Turn your phone and other electronic devices off, and remove any additional distractions. Once you have put yourself into that environment, I want you to do the following three simple things (read them all in full before you start to do them):

ONE: Close your eyes and take a few deep breaths.

TWO: Think of a moment in your life when you felt deeply proud. This could be a promotion you got yesterday or a science fair project you completed in fourth grade. Only you know what this moment is. With your eyes closed, decide what this moment is; try on a couple of possible "Hey, look what I did" moments for size. When you start to feel proud all over again, as though it were happening right now, you'll know you found the right moment.

THREE: With your eyes still closed, spend some time reliving that memorable moment over and over again. Take some time to re-experience all the positive emotions you associate with it. Feel yourself becoming even more deeply grateful for this experience.

Do those three things right now. When you are done, come back to the book.

WELCOME BACK!

If you have followed my instructions in this chapter, you have changed your paradigm. You made a commitment. You scheduled a personal session with your most important person—you—and you have held your first session and gained a mindfulness benefit from it.

Not only that—you now have access to your own personal remote control. You can use the experience you've just rediscovered as "gratitude fuel" *whenever* you encounter an obstacle that makes you feel overwhelmed or stressed out.

Well done!

SOFTWARE UPDATES

> Please remember: Your time is the most valuable time of all. With that principle in mind, begin the habit of scheduling, and creating, private sessions for yourself... with yourself. Today, take action to begin building up an expanding daily presence of "you time."

> You have the power to change your outcomes and your life. Change the channel and experience success in your mind. Let the experience rejuvenate and motivate you during your session with yourself.

> Whether you want success in this program or to achieve specific goals, being and staying committed will increase your chances of success by as much as 90 percent! Use your time to reinforce that commitment and your constructive AutoThoughts!

PROGRESSIVE JUMPS

> If you have not already done so, close your eyes and practice visualizing the positive event or memory we discussed in this chapter. Don't forget to be grateful for the experience.

> Schedule "you time" on your calendar to implement Days 6 through 14 of this program. Up until now, you have made a daily time investment into this program. As you formalize and deepen your commitment to it, you should gradually increase your daily time investment. Block off on your calendar the specific times you plan to invest in "you time." The time investments you schedule should increase a little bit each day for Days 6 through 14.

> You will be surprised at the lifelong return that even a small time investment in yourself can bring!

> As a reinforcement tool, you can now listen to "Day Five" in the audio support program.

UPDATE YOUR INTERNAL SOFTWARE

"The fuel you feed your mind
creates your reality."

THIS IS A BIG DAY... the day you and I have been working toward. Today, we'll be looking at the heart of this program. On previous days, we have been prepping your awareness, getting your mind in a receptive state through relaxation techniques and a practice of gratitude, and carving out dedicated time for the mindset work to come. Today, we will begin the process of updating your internal software. I think you'll find, as so many of my clients have, that it is the ultimate resource for performance, productivity, and prosperity.

By the way, if you happen to be the leader of a team or an organization, pay close attention, because this is extremely applicable to you. If you complete this program in its entirety and, once you are finished, share it with those who report to you, coaching them as necessary along the way, you will see that it has the potential to transform not only your own ability to achieve your professional goals, but your entire team's ability to accomplish their goals, as well. By making this one element of the program an integral part of your organization's culture, a daily part of "how we do things around here," you will unleash breakthroughs, both on the team and individual level, that you never imagined possible.

Corporate executives and business owners know the importance of improvement. Even those companies that are doing well are constantly striving to do and be better. They update their equipment and systems. They continually update their software, ensuring that they have the most current program versions. These companies update their internal systems, goals, and plans on a regular basis.

People also need to update their internal software. Our mindset is always working—*always*. It is like an app that runs in our brains continually. It never stops. However, it relies on the last or most dominant instructions it has been given—specifically, the last or most dominant thoughts, beliefs, and emotions it has received. Many of the beliefs and thoughts that guide our actions and goals are decades old. Some no longer serve us at all. They are outdated and, as a result, can slow or halt our progress and stifle our goals. By updating your internal software, you are writing new instructions for your mindset to work from.

In order to update your internal software, you must first decide what it is that you want. Do you want to build confidence or achieve a lifelong goal? Maybe your goal is to shave strokes off your golf game or lose weight. You might want to learn and master a new skill or overcome a fear. What are your dreams?

Are you aware of the thoughts that you feed your mind? The process of updating your internal software will maximize your greatest asset—you—by increasing your awareness and helping your mind focus on the results you want.

YOUR UPDATED APP

Updating your internal software will provide you with the tools you need to support your success. The best way to do this is to create a blueprint, in writing, of what you want to accomplish. Think of it as an app that contains a written list of your activities, thoughts, goals, and dreams. Like a journal, it is personal and intended for only you to see.

It is important that this list be in writing. It is your career blueprint, your happiness blueprint, and your life blueprint. You wouldn't attempt to construct a home without a blueprint. Similarly, your written list is a step-by-step plan that you refine and update daily so that you can create the changes you want in your life.

Don't be frightened by that word *journal*, which a lot of people associate with grade-school teachers and writing assignments they didn't particularly enjoy. This is not homework. This type of journaling is entirely what you make of it. It can be as extensive or as bare-bones as you want it to be, and nobody will be correcting your writing ability or looking for words you spelled wrong. As part of your "me time," this writing is just for you.

Your updated app can be written on your phone, in a note-book, or in a document on your computer. The words you write down might end up taking the form of a simple daily log, a series of longer diary entries, or even your memoirs. But like a grocery list that contains the items you need and want, it should always start with a list of the things you need and want in life.

Why is it so important that you put your list, your blueprint, in writing? The writing in our journals can be compared to thinking out loud. It is our internal thoughts and monologues recorded on paper. Therefore, journaling becomes a process of self-discovery that enables us to become aware of our conscious thoughts. In turn, this reinforces our thoughts, making them stronger and more consistent. When we include our goals in our writing, it solidifies and strengthens them. For this reason, it is important to focus on constructive thoughts, not destructive thoughts.

Writing is strongly correlated with success in achieving goals. A study by Dominican University of California professor Dr. Gail Matthews found that when goals are written down, they are 42 percent more likely to be achieved.[5] Success rates continue to increase even more if goals are vividly described in writing.

Two things happen when you write things down. First, you are giving yourself a visual reminder, something you can access and refer to often. The more you see it, the more it will be remembered. Second, neuropsychologists have found that when we write things down, we have greater memory and recall. By generating the written words ourselves, rather than reading someone else's writing, we are more likely to remember them—and in greater detail. This is called the "generation effect."

Here is a good example. In a study, job interviewers who took notes while interviewing applicants were 23 percent more likely to remember details about the interviewee than those who didn't take any notes at all. So the next time you sit in an interview, appreciate the fact that someone is taking notes, because they will be more likely to remember you and what makes you uniquely qualified for the position.

We already do this before we go to the grocery store. We make a list to ensure that we don't forget anything. If we don't, we risk that what we want or need will get overshadowed by distractions and choices. Writing a list helps us remember these needs and wants, and it really works...even if we forget to take the list with us. The act of writing the list itself etches the items onto our subconscious, so if we happen to forget the list, we can usually recall the items we wrote down...and often in the same order in which they were written.

The same principle applies to your success blueprint: writing a list of what you want and need in life will make those things more prominent in your mind. That way, the noise and busyness of the everyday will not cause you to ransack the impulse "shopping" traps and end up with a bunch of mental "junk" in your mindset. You have created a subconscious grocery list, which becomes a contract with your mindset to secure those most-desired items so that your thoughts and actions align with your guiding list—even when it's not physically in front of you. Because it is in writing, you are more likely to be attentive to it; it is like an app that is constantly running in your brain, helping you design and create what you want in life.

SEE YOUR POTENTIAL

Regardless of the style or content you choose, your list must be, first and foremost, a way to distract yourself from stress, tension, and temporary setbacks. When executed properly, you'll find that this list brings clarity and definition to new goals and passions. By creating this list, you can see your own potential. And it's the very best part of your "me time."

Writing this list should be simple and relaxing. That's requirement number one. If you follow that principle, you will find that the process of writing your goals, whether they are personal or professional, is one of the best ways to positively reinforce them and boost your confidence that you can and will achieve them.

Because writing is scientifically proven to be strongly linked to success, I want you to make it part of your daily routine. Writing this list is something you will do every day, starting today and continuing through Day 14…and beyond, as you should keep up with this practice long after you finish this program. Once you have a few weeks of journaling built up, you will be able to review your writing and see how you've grown and evolved. You'll have a chronicle of your progress toward your goals.

At the end of this chapter, I will share simple instructions to help you get started. Commit four or five minutes a day to jotting down your goals and aspirations. You will start with positively stated aspirations, but you won't limit yourself to that. Feel free to explore your innermost thoughts and capture those on paper, too. You will address questions like: *What made me happy today?*

What will make me happy tomorrow? What do I like about my life, and what, if anything, would I change for the better if I could?

PUTTING TOGETHER YOUR UPDATED APP

Updating your internal software is the process of creating a written list of the thoughts, beliefs, and accomplishments you want in your life. As you just learned, the action of writing actually increases your awareness. What do you want to change in your life? In what areas do you want to improve? Are the things you want personality traits, like courage, or are they possessions, like a new car? Do you want to eliminate bad habits or develop new, more positive ones? Regardless of what your list encompasses, this is going to be a mental blueprint that provides the structure for achieving your vision of success and fulfillment. You will create and review this mental blueprint daily, scheduling time each day for it in your calendar. Remember, if you do this, you are 42 percent more likely to get the results you want than if you don't put it in writing. You will start this process today, using the instructions at the end of this chapter.

Once you've honestly assessed and written down exactly what you want and the specific changes you'd like to create, you've begun the process of updating your awareness app. Even when that list isn't in front of you, you'll be able to recall what's on it and recreate it as circumstances require, like the shopper who forgot their list. The list will be there in your mind, because your subconscious stored it. As you focus, your subconscious returns it to you, reminding you of your intentions and goals and reinforcing why they are important to you. The list's mere existence will cause your conscious mind to act on it...and connect you with the things that will help you create whatever you wrote down. In essence, the list functions as an update to your internal software, which is constantly operating in your mind.

The process of updating your mindset gives you the ability to remove outdated goals, ideas, beliefs, and emotions and replace them with updated, positive goals, beliefs, and desires. By writing these things down, you are reinforcing them in your mind and making them a dominant part of your thought process. When you encounter opportunities, your current internal software— your mindset—will run from your updated app to bring you what you want. This is truly a game-changing tool for individuals, teams, and leaders. Take advantage of it, both personally and professionally.

The key here is consistency. You need to review your list every day! You'll get better and better at this as you define, refine, and rewrite your goals over time.

SOFTWARE UPDATES

> Your updated mental software is the ultimate resource for performance, productivity, and prosperity.

> Writing down your thoughts, emotions, and goals cements them in your subconscious grocery list, reinforcing them and making them easier to remember.

> Written goals are 42 percent more likely to be achieved.

> Journaling is an excellent discovery tool. It can help you express your emotions and define your priorities. When written positively, these feelings and goals serve as constructive AutoThoughts that become even stronger through the process of writing and reviewing them.

PROGRESSIVE JUMPS

> Continue to do the daily relaxation activities we discussed on Day 2.

> Schedule time to write and review your journal or goal list in your daily calendar. Do this for today and then for Days 7 through 14.

> Have fun with this process. Write your list in your notebook, journal, phone, or computer. Be as general or as specific as you want about the things you are creating in your life and the things you want to change for the better. Change is always available to us, and we have a choice in everything we do. This list is part of that process. You can change any part of your life at will, and

you can always use the gift of choice to point your life in whatever direction you choose. List each and every item you can think of, regardless of how important it might seem to someone else. If it is important to you, include it on the list. Remember, this is your life, and your list is your script. Everything you write is being recorded not only in that document, but also in your subconscious.

> Your list doesn't have to be complicated, but the more specific it is, the better. Just make sure it reflects your innermost thoughts and desires and that you are enjoying the process of recording them. I've included some suggestions below to help you get started, but don't worry if your list looks nothing at all like these suggestions. That's fine. Your script will be as personal and unique as you are. Important: Be sure that you state these aspirations in a POSITIVE, PRESENT-TENSE voice, as though the event or achievement is taking place RIGHT NOW.

> Examples of personal suggestions that you might use in your list include:

- I have less stress in my life.
- I reach out and engage effectively with other associates, colleagues, and others in your network.
- I take action quickly on important opportunities that come my way.

- I am confident.

- I am a solution provider to my customers.

- I listen to others and appreciate my relationships.

- I build on my skills and expertise. I meet and exceed my sales goals.

- I am healthy and physically fit.

- I am a happier person.

- I am grateful.

> You can create the same type of mental blueprint for calming your mind or for anything else that is important to you. Reducing stress, tension, and anxiety is, like everything else, an ongoing process of nurturing your mindset. Treat your mind like a garden. If you neglect your garden and don't tend to it, the weeds will grow and take over. Your mindset is the same way. You have to get rid of the items that don't belong there—the negativity, self-doubt, and previous beliefs that no longer serve you or your goals—so that the things you want in your subconscious garden can grow and be more productive and effective. I find that the more often I write my list, the better and more often I'm able to recall it. That's why I suggest making a new list at least once a week. It helps to reinforce it in your subconscious. Every time you write your list, you're reinforcing your belief that it can

become your reality—you're updating your mindset so that it can operate at its optimal level. You don't have to be in a state of deep relaxation to update the software that operates your mind and your life. The very act of doing, writing, or saying anything places and reaffirms a positive, constructive suggestion in your mind. When you're writing your personal list for the second and subsequent times, be sure to eliminate the items that aren't working for you and become more focused on the ones that are. Occasionally add new ones. Over time, you will become clearer and more focused on precisely what you want, and you will be able to visualize it in greater detail. Your subconscious will know exactly what you want and will automatically work to bring that to fruition.

❯ As a reinforcement tool, you can now listen to "Day Six" in the audio support program.

REINFORCEMENT

"Be fully conscious and present, and you can
tune into the guidance of your deepest mind."

ACCOMPLISHMENTS, large and small, give us a feeling
of purpose. They validate our efforts and success. I am a big fan of
celebrating and appreciating. Regardless of the achievement, it is
important to recognize it. Connecting with a new client, helping
an associate, or staying on track with a personal goal are accomplishments that you should celebrate.

Day 7 is a reinforcement day, an opportunity to apply what
you've already learned so that you can execute it more easily and
intuitively. The concept you're going to be reinforcing, applying,
and executing today is the transformative idea of updating your
awareness app.

My challenge to you today is to keep strengthening the muscle
of writing and reinforcing your updated app in your daily life. I
want you to find at least one area where you can point to a changed
behavior, a new outcome, or a specific goal you've achieved that

is linked directly to the list you created on Day 6. Case in point: A friend who is a writer used this technique to visualize himself, on a daily basis, finishing an important project. He thought he was at least two weeks away from completing it. However, by writing his list and reinforcing it in his mind, he was able to finish it at a high level of quality in just 48 hours!

That's the power of the technique we're talking about here. And that's what I want you to do for yourself today. Keep working on your list; keep using it to upgrade your beliefs, your actions, and your outcomes; and notice when you get a different result. Today, you will create the first chapter of your own personal success story.

THE POWER OF FIXATION

There is a special power that comes with using the list activity to focus your attention on something that's truly important to you. I call this the Power of Fixation. To harness it, we need to grasp that our brains will inevitably work very, very hard to fulfill our own thought processes, our own fixations. Our brains will look, look some more, and keep looking for a way to validate whatever fixation we have fed into it. The only catch is, we have to be careful what we fixate on. Whatever we ask for, we will get, whether that's positive or negative.

Consider someone who habitually complains about having bad luck on the job, at home, in the economy—basically everywhere. We've all met someone like that. Can you think of someone at work who never seems to run out of things to complain about? Someone who always seems to start the day by complaining about the traffic, or the weather, or how much work they have to do? Have you ever noticed that this person has no shortage of evidence to point to in support of the idea that "bad luck" has taken over their life? What's really happened is that this person has consistently chosen to dump negativity into their brain. That's what they fixate on. That's what they feed into their brain. So that's what the brain validates and brings into existence in their life. That's how powerful the human brain is!

I meet many people who respond to the life-changing principles I've shared with you by saying, directly or indirectly, "You know what? This stuff is great. I get it. It's very interesting. But I'm not really sure it's for me. I guess I'm just not that kind of person." Guess what? They're right. What they're fixating on when they say and think those things is, "I'm not the kind of person who takes action on opportunities to change my world and my life for the better." That's how they've chosen to program their brain. Therefore, that's what the brain validates for them.

Research has shown that people who focus on positive goals and thoughts are more creative and less likely to give up. In fact, research from Lyubomirsky, King, and Diener revealed that positive emotions result in higher productivity and higher ratings in performance reviews.[6] Moreover, optimists are three times more likely to have good performance ratings than pessimists. Their brain validates what they feel strongest about and what they focus on the most.

YOU ARE ALWAYS UPDATING YOUR AWARENESS APP

Yesterday, we formalized the process of writing down your goal list, because doing so is an extremely powerful and effective way to take control of the Power of Fixation. But you know what? We are all creating goals, dreams, and thoughts in our mind all the time, whether we write them down or not and whether we realize that's what we're doing or not. We also learned yesterday that it's much better when we do it consciously…but regardless, we do it all the time. We update that list constantly, often in a way that doesn't support us.

I have people tell me things like, "Oh, I could never get in front of an audience and give a speech." Guess what just happened? That person just updated and reinforced a long-standing belief on his or her mental list. Whenever I hear something like that, I'm tempted to say, "Nope. You're right. You can't. You just made sure of that. Tell me what else you want, because you've already figured out how to fulfill that particular goal—not speaking in front of an audience—with absolute mental clarity. What's next on the list? What else do you not want to be able to do?"

I realize that's a little harsh, but I share that response with you for a reason. We all have clutter on our "default" mental lists. You. Me. Everyone. The trick is becoming aware of the destructive AutoThoughts that are sabotaging you and flipping the script on them to turn them into gold. And that's actually surprisingly easy to do.

Today, I want you to notice the clutter on your default list, the prewritten and outdated app you've fed your mind, including the negative feelings, assumptions, and messaging that come up automatically. For instance, if you're a salesperson, the junk on your mental list might sound like this:

> ❯ "I hate cold calling."
> ❯ "I can't get through to decision makers."
> ❯ "I'll never be as successful as Jim."
> ❯ "I feel like I'm overwhelmed by the job of selling. I always feel tired and worn out by the middle of the day."
> ❯ "There's never enough hours in the day for me to get everything done that I need to get done."

I want you to really notice these specific bits of junk on your default list, and rewrite them so that they turn into positives that you can record, and reinforce, on your conscious awareness app. For instance:

> ❯ "I am creative enough to find new prospects."
> ❯ "I enjoy building relationships and offering solutions to decision makers. Reaching the right ones is easy."
> ❯ "I am as successful as anyone on the team."
> ❯ "There is always time and energy for me to move forward on my goals."

Get the idea? Use your junk thinking to create positive elements on your list, and use today to start creating actual results that can serve as evidence in support of those constructive beliefs.

For instance, if one of the clutter elements on your default list happens to be "I have rotten luck," notice that...and then turn that junk into gold! Make sure you write down something like "I am grateful for the tangible abundance and opportunity that I enjoy and take action on every day," and then be sure to reinforce that belief at key points during your day!

You know what's going to happen when you do that? You're going to start NOTICING instances of tangible abundance and opportunity that come your way during the day...and you're going to start acting on them!

Like a computer program, your mindset responds to the commands you give it—but it does so according to the pathways enabled by its coding. If the pathways you've created through the coding tend toward destructive ends, then your brain will instantly and enthusiastically process inputs in that direction. On the other hand, if you update your mental app so that you reverse the direction of your pathways from negative to positive, your brain will just as easily facilitate your success. So, for example, if your internal software has been programmed to operate on the belief that you can't get out of debt, then your brain will facilitate actions that reinforce that idea: you'll spend more, you'll avoid repayments, etc. However, if you update your app with the coding of "I am taking the steps necessary to get out of debt," your brain will reinforce pathways that process inputs in that direction. It's all a question of what you want your mindset to do, what commands you give it, and how you choose to reinforce the behaviors.

The big question for you right now—and every day of your life moving forward, even after you finish this book—is a simple one: What do you want your brain to do? What realities do you want it to manifest for you? What experiences do you want it to point you toward? What doors do you want it to open for you?

Use today to get some real clarity on that...and to get some victories under your belt.

But don't forget that when you do, you need to reinforce them. Celebrate your victories. Reward yourself. Let positive reinforcement increase your focus on and attentiveness to what you want. Soon, you will find that automatically, without thinking, you have adopted and are regularly acting on the items on your list, even when you aren't aware of it.

SOFTWARE UPDATES

> Reinforcements make things stronger. This is true with thoughts, emotions, achievements, and goals. It is true for both positive and negative things. Focus on reinforcing the positive items in your updated awareness app to make them the strongest instructions in your mind.

> Make a conscious effort to identify negative thoughts and beliefs. Then counter them with positive affirmations

that support what you want. Make sure you write those affirmations on your revised list, which updates your awareness app.

> Reward yourself for every achievement, no matter how small. Celebrations and rewards reinforce our results and spur the brain to continue to bring more of the same.

PROGRESSIVE JUMPS

> ACT! Do your relaxation activities.

> In addition to engaging in your relaxation activities, I want you to notice a specific piece of negative mental imagery or assumption in your own mind…reverse it…build its positive counterpart into the coding of your awareness app…and then find a way to celebrate your achievement whenever you take advantage of even a tiny chance to turn a new affirmation into a reality in your life.

> Don't wait for a monumental success to start celebrating the victories you manifest. Celebrate the incremental victories, too!

> As a reinforcement tool, you can now listen to "Day Seven" in the audio support program.

VISUALIZE

"Control your results by gaining control of your thoughts. Inspire within!"

WELCOME BACK! If you're following the schedule, you spent yesterday reinforcing your awareness app and celebrating your progress. You got personal and specific with the items you programmed into your awareness app, you revised that list and made it uniquely yours, and you found a reason to celebrate a victory, even a small victory, in turning affirmations into reality.

Now you are ready to move on to one of the most powerful strategies in your arsenal.

You've already discovered the power of visualization to create a state of relaxation. Today, you learn to use this tool to actively construct the life you want. You'll begin to leverage mental images that support you, make you happy, and attract success into your life. Once you become skilled at building strong pictures that register in your subconscious, like the best professional athletes do, the possibilities are unlimited.

THE POWER OF MENTAL IMAGERY

Mental pictures are incredibly powerful, because any visualization that is held and repeated in your mind frames the way you think. Whatever you surround yourself with visually has extraordinary power to guide your thoughts. As a practical matter, I can tell you that your thoughts—and your performance, for that matter—will not make a powerful shift toward the next level of achievement until you expose them to different pictures.

One of the powerful aspects of visualization is that images direct your mind, telling it which things to focus on. The more detailed the visualization, the more you will focus and concentrate on your mental image. Olympian Michael Phelps practices visualization every morning and every night. Not only does he rehearse his performance in his mind, but he takes it up another notch and imagines a perfect performance!

Professional athletes like Phelps know the power of visualization. If you think back to a time you've been watching television and you've seen a top-tier athlete preparing for an event, you saw them close their eyes for several minutes. A skier doing this, for example, is likely visualizing gliding down that slope, maneuvering around the poles, and following the course in their mind. When it comes time to physically execute the same thing, they know every turn and every slope of the hill because they've done it 10 times already in their mind. Athletes who use visualization in this way have been shown to outperform athletes who don't.

Similarly, visualization can be a powerful tool in accomplishing personal or professional goals. Visualizing success in a job interview or a contract negotiation will strongly prepare you and give you confidence. Visualizing meeting a new client and making a sales pitch will give new salespeople much-needed experience and a higher comfort level than they would otherwise have. Imagining yourself as you give a presentation in its entirety or a speech in front of a large audience will help you overcome fears and boost your confidence. Salespeople and executives can visualize their goals and, therefore, increase the likelihood of achieving them faster. If you want a new car or a bigger paycheck, visualization will keep your focus—and thus, your actions—directed toward that goal so you can make it happen.

Why does this work so well? Let me answer that question by posing another: Do you ever talk to yourself? Perhaps you don't want to admit it, or perhaps you don't even realize you're doing it, but the truth is that every human being has an internal monologue—whether or not they voice these thoughts out loud is another question. Humans have a sixth sense—an "extra sense" into which all the other sensory modalities feed—that we don't usually acknowledge. This extra sense is the means by which an individual forms his or her own unique perceptions, emotions, actions, and responses to situations. This special sense is what makes us human and gives us our individuality. This special sense is what frames our thoughts and our reality. It is massively underutilized. And visualization is the single best way to get the most from it.

I am referring to your INNER VOICE!

Your Inner Voice is something you can benefit from at any time of the day or night. It works in conjunction with your Mind's Eye—your internal vision that associates stored images with other sensory inputs—to construct your reality. For instance, if you're feeling stressed, you can find a quiet place, close your eyes, and use your Inner Voice to turn the situation around. Harness the power of visualization by describing to yourself a stress-free environment, such as a warm, sandy beach, that make you happy. Guess what happens? By building and experiencing strong, powerful, positive pictures using your Inner Voice, you point the awesome power of your mindset toward the outcome you desire: a stress-free response to your world. You can do this with any situation. The possibilities are jaw-dropping! That's why pro athletes—and indeed, high-achieving people in virtually every field—rely on the Inner Voice, even though they may not call the process by that name.

Visualization plays a very important part in creating our mindset. Our Inner Voice constructs mental images that function the same way as external visual inputs—our brain does not distinguish between fabricated and "actual" images. When our Mind's Eye sees something, even if it's not "real," we begin to believe it. That vision then becomes more real for us, and attaining it becomes more achievable. Our internal monologue shifts as a result, and the process begins again—but this time, the Inner Voice is operating at a higher level to manifest more abundance through subsequent visualizations.

How does this work? Well, while our brains are fascinating and complex, they are also simple and reliable. The human brain has been studied extensively, and multiple studies show that visualization works because the brain cannot tell the difference between real memories and those that are imagined. To the brain, they are one and the same. And the brain will respond to each in the same way. What does that mean? It means you can imagine a particular situation or experience, and the brain interprets and records it as a memory, even though it wasn't real. So when you do face that situation or experience in the future, the brain treats it as if you've already done that, giving you more focus and confidence. Your brain thinks your visual images are possible because it has already experienced them.

Imagine that you have a fear of flying. You visualize the experience of going to the airport and boarding a plane. You imagine takeoff and construct the sensation of a calm, peaceful feeling while in flight. You descend and smile as you land safely. The brain records this visualization as a real memory, so when you have an opportunity to fly in the future, you will feel less fear because your brain responds by believing not only that you've done this before, but that the experience was relaxing and enjoyable.

When I work with people in private coaching sessions to help them overcome challenges and realize their full potential, I always ask them to focus on an object or image that is calming to them. As they focus on this mental picture, I ask them to describe it in detail, along with the sensations they experience as they interact with it: sight, sound, touch, taste, and smell, if applicable. Then, I ask them to transfer these sensations to an experience that currently lacks a positive valuation in their mind. As they visualize this experience that has caused them anxiety, fear, upset, anger, etc., they narrate their interactions with it using the sensory and emotional language attached to the calming object or image. The result is that the negative experience becomes revalued as a positive one. This is the power of the Inner Voice when paired with the Mind's Eye. By using your internal monologue in tandem with visualization, we can direct our thoughts and suggestions to relax ourselves and then guide us toward something we desire.

Our mindset is the most powerful tool we possess. The concept behind using your Inner Voice is that the body and the mind are connected to each other. Our body responds to emotions, smells, tastes, sounds, and the things we see. Your Inner Voice works around the belief that our mind will also respond to the things we visualize, even if they're not real.

This strategy has been used successfully to promote healing by visualizing one's body free of pain or injury, to prepare us for stressful events, to quit smoking, to lose weight, and even to serve as a guide to help find solutions to the major problems we face in life, like dealing with the loss of a loved one. People also use positive visualizations and suggestions in preparation for surgery or during childbirth. If you use language to construct a vivid mental image with attendant sensory experiences, your thoughts will change, your beliefs will change, and as a result, the way you experience the world will change.

Your Inner Voice puts you in the driver's seat. You really can choose the suggestions and visualizations you want to experience in life and turn them into realities. You can choose your desired outcome. The direction you take is entirely up to you.

Your Inner Voice can bring you the things you really want in life, whether you're looking for a change in health, attitude, performance, or well-being. When you use it to relax, your Inner Voice can improve your physical health by reducing anxiety, lowering blood pressure, or promoting a good night's sleep. You can use your Inner Voice to improve your professional performance by painting a picture of you successfully meeting a sales quota, completing a major project, or troubleshooting a problem. It's like a dress rehearsal, a practice of sorts, which prepares you for the actual task. You can use it to create a mental dress rehearsal for any truly worthwhile goal or aspiration. It's your voice—use it to drive your success!

There are many practices that employ variations of the guided imagery technique that lies at the heart of using your Inner Voice that I will be sharing with you today and in the days ahead. One is the simple strategy of creating a note on your desktop and posting pictures or photographs of the things you want, which you then look at several times a day. Eventually, you find that the things depicted in those images begin to become a part of your reality. Every time you look at them, the images are recorded and reinforced in your subconscious, which updates your mindset. Just like with your list of goals and aspirations, even when you aren't looking at one of these images, you will find that you can recall exactly what it was that you wanted to achieve or acquire, what it looked like, and how you'll feel when you finally make it a reality. This is a powerful "add-on" to the awareness app—and by the way, it's something that a lot of corporate teams use to enhance motivation for both individual and team goals.

Visualization works. By visualizing yourself thinner, being thinner seems more attainable, and your mind responds as it keeps that goal strong and prominent during the day. A picture of the house or car of your dreams will also serve as a daily incentive to your subconscious to work in the direction of your goals. The more you see what you want, the more your subconscious mind will cause your conscious mind to seek ways to bring it to you.

Using your Inner Voice is the process of giving your mind suggestions that cause your body and emotions to respond as if you were experiencing what you want in your current reality. If the mind can perceive it, it can believe it. Once your mind believes what your Inner Voice enables your Mind's Eye to see, the sky is the limit!

SOFTWARE UPDATES

> The Inner Voice can control the script that runs your mindset app. You can maximize its efficacy by pairing it with the Mind's Eye and using language to construct positive mental images on which you can focus and manifest in your life.

> Visualization and guided imagery are as effective for improving results as skills-based practice. They boost confidence and act like a mental dress rehearsal, giving us experience and heightened performance.

> Images can improve our focus and concentration, directing our mind toward the things we visualize.

> The mind treats both real and imagined experiences and feelings the same. It cannot tell the difference between them. Guided imagery and visualization provide your mind with a powerful new reality that will enable you to overcome your fears, reduce your stress, and accomplish your goals.

PROGRESSIVE JUMPS

> Take a few minutes today to do the following:

- Imagine a lemon or a really sour pickle. Picture it in your mind by describing the juices and how they smell and taste when you take that first bite. Can you taste how sour, tart, or salty it is? Are your senses responding to the visualization, causing you to salivate or pucker? If so, you've just experienced one way your body responds to guided imagery. If a visualization or thought can cause the body to anticipate or crave a specific food, doesn't it seem logical that the mind can also be used to influence the way our body responds to other things, like pain, stress, or anxiety?

- Now that you have experienced it for yourself, begin thinking about specific ways you can use the Inner Voice to generate mental imagery to enhance the quality of your daily life. I'll give you some more ideas about this tomorrow, but in preparation for Day 9, write down your own ideas about how you can leverage the power of your Inner Voice in your world.

> As a reinforcement tool, you can now listen to "Day Eight" in the audio support program.

REFINING YOUR AWARENESS APP

"Opportunities present themselves when we change the way we perceive the world around us."

TODAY, YOU WILL FOCUS on your list of goals, your awareness app. You will refine it, update it, and evaluate what works best for you. In doing so, you will gain clarity about exactly what it is you want. In turn, you will begin to strengthen your reinforcement of that list with a deeper level of personalized visualization. When that happens, you will find yourself taking consistent action to make your Inner Voice your personal ally as your awareness application is developed to its full potential.

This stage of the process is truly remarkable! I have witnessed people I have worked with make powerful, positive changes in their lives when they make the choice to refine their awareness app. It is all about customizing the life you want so that it fits you and only you and then continually tailoring it so that it is adjusted to your specific needs in every stage of your growth. Today, you will discover how to refine your awareness app to achieve the goals you have mapped out for yourself.

COMMIT AND MAKE INCREMENTAL PROGRESS EVERY DAY

Harnessing the immense, untapped power of your own thoughts takes patience, time, and determination to succeed. It is a daily process of transformation that creates a strong desire and the motivation to take action toward your achievements. The more you practice it, repeat it, and believe it, the clearer your goals become! As your goals continue to solidify, you will realize your potential to achieve them.

A Harvard MBA study regarding goal setting shows us just how important this process is. They found that 84 percent of the class they studied had no goals at all. Only 13 percent had goals and had written them down—in other words, they had created an awareness app and put it in writing so they could see it and refer to it often. Just 3 percent of this class had both written goals and actual plans to achieve them. The participants were followed over a course of ten years, and the study revealed that the 13 percent who had written goals were making twice as much money as the 84 percent who didn't, and the 3 percent who had written goals and a plan were making ten times as much as all of them![7]

Utilize what I call the three R's when considering what your awareness app encompasses: *revisiting, reinforcing,* and *revising.*

This allows you to continually monitor, track, and adjust your goals to make sure they always fit and are always aligned with your desires.

Positive results are within your reach, and they are tailor-made just for you. Persevering creates positive results. You cannot reach any destination if you stop trying to get there. The same is true for the changes you want to make—those changes are possible only if you continue to make progress toward their achievement. The end goal is to create steady, incremental progress for these 14 days…and every day that follows.

Yes, there will be setbacks from time to time. You will get distracted and sidetracked. You might find that you need to revise your awareness app so that it stays relevant to your life and needs. That's okay, and it is an important part of the process. You might even find that there are times when you don't think it's working and become discouraged. If that happens, dig your heels in a little deeper and stay committed to the process.

Let me introduce you to Anthony, who purchased my stop-smoking audio album. Anthony and I met, and he mentioned that he had listened to the program the night before… and was frustrated that it "had not worked" for him the very next day!

I pointed out that, yes, there are individuals who have an immediate response to my program…but for others, it may take a little more time. That surprised him—he thought he could listen to it one time and then stop smoking forever. The piece of the process he was misunderstanding was repetition.

I encouraged him to give the program a chance and not to make any judgments until he listened to all the affirmations and completed all the relaxation exercises for one week. I asked Anthony to give feedback on his progress at the end of the week.

Guess what? Simply by choosing to commit to the program and making it part of his regular routine, Anthony successfully quit smoking! Sometimes that is the simplest—and best—refinement of your awareness app: owning what you are responsible for and fine-tuning it to perfection.

Over the course of that week, Anthony came to realize that, no matter how much I could help him, ultimately he was the one who had to focus consistently on his goal. I couldn't do that for him. I couldn't be with him to reinforce the suggestions in his mind. He had to translate the program's affirmations into powerful motivators that changed his actions. He had to own his goal list, and he needed to stay with it. Once he did, his awareness and his thinking changed.

Like Anthony, the changes you want to create probably won't occur overnight, but if you stay committed I assure you that they will happen. You—and only you—are accountable for your results. You are the only one who has the power to change the thoughts you are feeding yourself. You are the one who must be receptive to your awareness app. And only you can make that app function behind the scenes to progress you toward what you want.

Notice, too, that Anthony was initially ready to declare this process a failure after the very first try…simply because he expected it to work immediately, without any effort on his part. Once he committed to a consistent approach and put forth a little effort, he got results very quickly. Once he accepted that this process isn't a sprint, but instead a marathon, all of the components became cohesive and productive. Like Anthony, you need to understand that this is a daily process that requires your participation. You cannot just create your goal list, your awareness app, and walk away. You need to make it yours, own it, and refine it so that it will continue to work for you.

As you're creating your awareness app update, I want you to own your goal list by committing to make it a part of your DAILY routine. That means relaxing into it, using the techniques I've shared with you, and then repeating the affirmations as part of a scheduled, regular routine.

Yes, I want you to actually schedule it for a specific time each day, just like an important appointment that you cannot and do not want to miss, and I want you to follow through. You are the one who will turn these visualizations into reality, not me! Doing a little bit every day is extremely important. If you wanted to use water to wear down a stone, would it be better to dump a bucket of water over the stone once and then walk away or to drip water on the stone consistently every day for a year? Clearly, the latter would be more effective. Similarly, it's impossible to lose 20 pounds in a day, but it is very possible to lose 20 pounds over a period of several months if you make a daily commitment to your goal and follow through every single day with healthy eating and exercise.

MASTERING SELF-TALK

A while back, my dear friend, Patti, shared a story with me about her first teaching job. She had absolutely no experience in public speaking, but she had been asked to be a part-time instructor at a community college, teaching computer programming. She was well versed in the subject, and she agreed to take on the task.

Patti prepared her first lesson, but when she got in front of the class, a case of severe stage fright overcame her. Her voice was shaking, she could tell that the students knew she was uncomfortable, and she lost her train of thought. She told me that she finally had to excuse herself from the classroom and go into the hall to calm down.

The words she spoke to herself saved her. "Come on, Patti, you can do this. These people are just like you; they're no different. Calm down. Relax. Focus on what you know." And as she focused on what she knew, she visualized herself delivering her class calmly and proficiently. After taking several deep breaths, she returned to the class and apologized, telling them it was her first time teaching and that she was a little nervous. She talked to the students and asked them to talk to her. Before long, they were more comfortable with each other. The first day of teaching was a success.

What did she do to make that happen? She took responsibility…and she visualized. She knew she had an obligation to teach the class and that she was accountable to those students. She knew that it was her responsibility to pull herself together and change her emotional state so that she could perform her duties.

Then she went into the hall and changed her negative self-talk into constructive thoughts, placing a suggestion in her own mind that she could stand in front of the class without being overcome by anxiety and reinforcing it with visualization.

Patti's Inner Voice changed the way she thought, felt, and reacted. It was her Inner Voice that gave her the courage to walk back into the classroom and admit to the students that she was nervous. Positive self-talk was the key to overcoming her fear. It's a powerful tool that reframes your mindset, and you can use it, too, in order to achieve what you want—whether you want to overcome a fear, reach a milestone, or achieve a goal.

Patti used my system that day, and she didn't even realize it. That's what's so powerful about these techniques. At some deep level, we already know they work…and we already know how to use them. It's just a question of whether we will take action to activate this knowledge at a very deep level. That is why today is such an important part of the process—it's all about bringing greater clarity to your awareness app and deepening your commitment to it on a daily basis.

Setting clear expectations, turning them into brief affirmations that are part of your awareness app (positive self-talk), and then visualizing the positive outcome you want will help you get closer to your goal. Patti set an expectation that she could go into that classroom and face those students. She told herself, "You *can* do this." She was aware of her problem and sought an answer to it. She saw herself relaxing and delivering her material. And then she did just that.

Self-talk is an important part of refining and reinforcing your awareness app so that it works for you. A study released by Ethan Kross, a psychology professor at the University of Michigan, revealed that the language we use in self-talk influences the way we feel, think, and behave. It has the power to make us feel better (or worse) about ourselves. The right words and reinforcement provide us with a boost of confidence that helps us overcome challenges and obstacles.[8]

Don't expect to create the change you want overnight. Again, Anthony had to stay committed to his daily exercises before they altered his actions. Patti was able to overcome the initial stress of public speaking with self-talk and visualization, but it took time for her to become comfortable in that position. By using the same techniques we've discussed in this program, though, they both were able to meet their individual goals. So can you.

What Patti and Anthony accomplished can be replicated and made relevant to almost anything. They didn't change anything outside of them—their accomplishments occurred within. It had to do with persistence, accountability, visualization, and sending the right messages to the subconscious mind.

You can't expect to lose 20 pounds in a week. You can't expect to earn a million dollars overnight. You can't become the top salesperson of the year in a single day or change the entire culture of an organization in one fell swoop. It requires attention, focus, repetition, and reinforcement. In other words, you have to change old habits and patterns of thinking consciously before you can replace them with new habits and patterns that will create the results you want. If you fail to give this conscious and committed effort, it will be too easy to fall back into old patterns and habits.

Have you ever attended a motivational keynote that had you excited and ready to commit to achieving your goals? You were pumped up and excited about making the changes you wanted. Initially, you had an "I can do it!" attitude and a strong desire to make it happen. However, as you returned to your regular routine, you were distracted from your goal and slid right back into your usual routine and previous thought patterns. Before you knew it, two weeks had passed, and not only had you not accomplished anything toward your goal, but you'd also lost your motivation and emotional connection to it.

That is why you have to master self-talk as you refine and execute your awareness app. It requires repetition and daily reminders to maintain your commitment, focus, and attention. You cannot make major changes in your life overnight. This is why you need to invest in yourself daily and set a specific time to do so on your calendar. The time can change as needed, but the commitment cannot! You can set realistic goals and take real action toward their achievement. Relax, focus, and give yourself the suggestion that you will improve your circumstances, enhance your career, and leverage your opportunities. Truly believe it. You might not get that overnight windfall of cash, but before long you'll find that the answers will come to you.

THE BACKSTAGE REQUEST

Let me tell you about Jonathan, the CEO of a worldwide company. His organization had hired me six times within a two-year period to speak at their conferences. The audiences ranged from sales teams to executives. By the time I was about to do the sixth event, Jonathan had heard incredible positive feedback from the programs and wanted to meet me personally. I was told that Jonathan would meet me backstage after my program, and sure enough, he was there when I walked off stage.

For about ten minutes, we spoke casually about how the events had gone and the overwhelming feedback from the audience members. I was humbled and grateful to receive this directly from him. Then Jonathan said, "I'd like to ask you a favor. Will you teach me a technique to help me have more confidence and remove my fear of presenting to very large groups?"

I was a bit surprised. I had been told that he was a great leader, a compelling speaker, and a very motivating person. However, it became clear that he personally struggled and had significant fear and anxiety about this issue. When Jonathan needed to prepare for a presentation in front of 100, 200, or 500 people, he spiraled. He started picturing himself failing in front of all those people and, as a result, did not perform at the level he wanted to.

I got a strange look when I said, "Jonathan, I can't do anything for you."

There was an uneasy pause. That response definitely wasn't what he had expected. Then I said, "I can show you the way, but you are going to have to do this for yourself."

He smiled. We got started.

We found a quiet room, and we spoke for another 30 minutes. I shared with him many of the same things I have shared with you in this book. I asked him to get back to me in several weeks, after his next presentation.

Following the same basic principles I have been outlining for you, Jonathan succeeded in changing his software—his thought processes. He is no longer paralyzed by fear when it's time to speak in front of a very large group. He is committed to taking time to make sure his thoughts and mental imagery are moving him in the right direction. He did this on his own and realizes he is in control now…not the preconceived outcome of nervousness or failure.

CHANGE YOUR AWARENESS APP

Given what you've just learned and all that you've put into practice on the previous days, I want you to work on revising your goal list and awareness app, as well as your whole attitude toward it.

For instance, if you are a salesperson, revise your awareness app to include a personalized affirmation like "I put people at ease," or "I deliver value to my customers and offer them solutions." Repeat it and reinforce it every single day. Your subconscious mind will point you toward the people, resources, and strategies you need to make those detailed statements realities!

Notice that this is not just *wishing* you were closing more sales. It's taking ownership of the content, frequency, and application of the messages and thoughts with which you are programming your mindset. Own it! Send yourself the right messages, because no one else is going to do that for you. Make sending this part of your daily routine…and then look for opportunities to take action! This is how you change the awareness app that is constantly running in your mind and directing your actions and outcomes.

You can't expect to increase sales without setting the right expectations and then doing something about those expectations. The same principle holds true for anything and everything you want to upgrade in life. You can't just *wish* that your relationships will improve and expect positive results; you must send yourself the right messages and then take steps that will actually improve your relationships.

You can always change and upgrade your awareness app… and you should. You will change. Your circumstances might change. But there is one thing that will always be consistent: you can always give yourself the power of belief. You can always start thinking, visualizing, and acting as though you are capable of achieving whatever you set your mind to do. You—and only you—will establish the limits on your experience through your thoughts, judgments, and actions.

Starting today, assume personal responsibility for revising and refining your awareness app. That's not my job. It's yours. I want you to become commander in chief of whatever you want most in life…and to report back only to yourself.

Today, *you* take control. Today, *you* are accountable. Today, *you* go out and make it happen.

SOFTWARE UPDATES

> Our mindset functions on the thoughts and beliefs it has been fed. It takes commitment and dedication to replace those thought and beliefs. Reinforce your new, updated beliefs (your awareness app) every day to avoid falling back into old patterns and habits.

> Review and update your awareness app every day to make sure it aligns with your current goals and desires. The more you do, the more your app will become fine-tuned and reinforced in your mind.

PROGRESSIVE JUMPS

> In addition to listening to the audio program and doing your normal relaxation activities, take time today to do the following things:

- Relabel and repurpose the scheduled time you have set aside for relaxation each day so that this time is now devoted to updating your awareness app.

- Write down a brand-new draft of your goals, or the script for your awareness app, personalizing it to what you want to be, do, or become, and revising it to take into account what you have learned and experienced firsthand since Day 1 of this program.

- Own your awareness app by committing to making it a part of your daily routine.

- Visualize specific positive outcomes.

- Expect gradual, incremental progress...and find a victory, big or small, to celebrate each day.

❯ As a reinforcement tool, you can now listen to "Day Nine" in the audio support program.

TRUST

"You—and you alone—are accountable for who you are, the decisions you make, and the actions you take. Once you accept that, everything else becomes easier, and you begin to build trust in yourself."

HERE'S A PARADOX TO CONSIDER: When we say, "I wish," we've already admitted that we can't.

> **"When we say, "I wish," we've already admitted that we can't.**

"I wish I was rich." "I wish I could lose 15 pounds." "I wish I could be a doctor." When you say that, you are admitting that you can't. Why can't you? The very first obstacle in your way is trust—or rather, a *lack* of trust. By saying, "I wish" instead of "I can," you've already verbally accepted that you cannot achieve those outcomes.

In this context, *wish* is a dirty word. It's a destructive word, rather than a constructive one—just like "I'll try," as we discussed on Day 3, is unproductive, whereas "I will" converts thoughts into actions.

The key to deleting "I wish," "I'll try," and similar ideas from your mental vocabulary—not just the words you speak, but the thoughts you think and the images you envision—is TRUST.

TRUST YOURSELF

Trust shows up in just about every critical human interaction. It's so important that it's printed and stamped on US currency ("In God we trust") and used as a basis for loans. Trust serves as the cornerstone of a solid foundation in any good relationship—personal, professional, or otherwise. We build so much on the basis of trust—partnerships, contracts, businesses, and marriages. But I believe the most essential use we can ever make of trust comes when we place it in ourselves.

Our ability to trust our own judgment, instincts, skills, and capabilities can be, and usually is, the deciding factor in how far we go in life, what we accomplish, and how happy and self-confident we are.

When you look within, take a deep breath, and trust yourself, good things happen. You're confident in your ability to make good decisions, produce, succeed, and achieve. But when that deep trust is absent, you hit a roadblock. You start saying and thinking things like "I wish" and "If only," which puts the screeching brakes on your desire, potential, and achievements. By saying "I wish" and "If only," you're really accepting the perceived outcome that what you want cannot and will not happen.

For example, assume you are meeting a new potential client. At the interview, you're asked if you're comfortable presenting new and innovative ideas to their company's movers and shakers. In reality, you've never felt comfortable speaking in front of a group, and deep down you don't trust your ability to meet this expectation satisfactorily.

How do you think you'd respond to the prospect's question? Would you forcefully assure the interviewer that you are competent and comfortable in this area? Maybe you would. Maybe you wouldn't. But most people who don't yet trust themselves to perform in such an area will, regardless of the words they choose to speak, show some hesitation in their tone, phrasing, and actions that exposes their lack of internal confidence to successfully carry out the responsibility.

The point is this: what we think—and specifically, what we think about ourselves—is reflected in everything we do and say. People can hear a lack of conviction and trust in our voice, they can see it in our body language, and they can feel it in the way we present ourselves. They base their level of trust in us on the level of trust we have in ourselves.

If the level of trust in ourselves affects other people to such an extent, how deeply must it affect us?

Deepening the level of trust in ourselves and our own instincts creates confidence, dedication, perseverance, and belief—all qualities that drive us toward achievement. A lack of trust in ourselves and our instincts, on the other hand, creates doubt, fear, anxiety, and an unwillingness to attempt anything—whether it be pursuing an education, changing jobs, making a commitment in a relationship, or attaining any worthy goal.

The lack of trust turns a goal into a wish. (There's that dirty, destructive four-letter word again.) Never forget: A wish is, by definition, something over which we have no power; it's a dream left to the stars and fate. Be realistic. How many wishes come true without any effort on our part? Few, if any!

TRUST IS NOT ARROGANCE

Some people hear what I have to say about trust and say, "Wait a minute. Are you saying I should pretend to myself and others that I know everything? That I can do everything? That I never make a mistake?"

Of course not.

Sure, there are skills we don't have. There's always something we don't know. But that doesn't mean that it's not possible to learn them. There's always a new challenge that takes us out of our comfort zone…but that doesn't mean we have to stay where we are and stop learning and growing. Here's the key question: Is your guiding internal assumption that you can master a new skill and face up to a challenge…or that you can't?

Growing and developing as a person is always a step-by-step process. It's about getting from where you are to where you want to be. Building trust in yourself is a giant leap toward creating a growth mindset. That's because positive change requires the self-confidence that you can achieve it. However, you can never have that inner confidence if you don't trust yourself.

Assuming that you will find a way to locate the answer you need is not the same as lying about your capabilities. It's not arrogance—it's initiative. When you stop to think about it, it makes complete sense. We trust total strangers with our money; we call them bankers. We trust people we don't personally know to take care of our children; we call them teachers. We trust individuals we just met with our health; they're our doctors. Yet we don't trust and have faith in our greatest asset, the one person we know the very best—ourselves.

We teach our children to believe they can be anything they want to be. We encourage and motivate them. We build up their self-confidence and self-esteem so they can grow up and face the world head-on. Yet we turn around and feed ourselves the exact opposite instructions! We don't try to lose weight because we're convinced it won't happen. *It hasn't worked before, and it won't happen this time, either.* We don't further our education and our personal development because we doubt our capabilities. We don't try to take ourselves to the next level in our career because we've already told ourselves we aren't qualified, experienced, or don't stand a chance. In these instances, it's easy to see that what we believe and say to ourselves has already determined the outcome…even before we begin.

Believing in yourself is the key to accomplishing anything of substance in life. Negative self-talk and visualizations destroy accomplishment. They even destroy the pursuit of accomplishment. We must retrain our mind to believe we can achieve the things we want, and we must build a relationship of trust with ourselves that's unshakable.

THE MOST POWERFUL
COACH IN THE WORLD

Whether you want to be a marathon runner, a million-dollar real estate investor, or salesperson of the year, you have to start out by trusting in your talent, skills, and ability. Many people turn to personal coaches to help them gain the skills they need but don't have—and even to help them improve and refine abilities they do have. For instance, a person who has been in the same position for a long time but who wants to—or has to—grow within their organization may go to a career coach for professional development advice.

Good coaches will help these people recognize the assets they already possess and show them how to present them in a way that will be attractive to a potential employer. The coach may also help the person distinguish between just any job offer and the right job offer. There are coaches available in almost any area of personal or professional development—financial coaches, marketing coaches, relationship coaches, physical training and fitness coaches, strategic coaches, voice coaches—the list goes on and on. These coaches not only teach us skills, but they keep us on track, motivating and encouraging us to attain the level of skill necessary to succeed.

But for most of us, hiring a coach is a one-time thing. Few of us have the resources to take our coach with us everywhere we go, like professional athletes do. At some point, we're left with only our personal resources. We're on our own. That's why we must remind ourselves to trust the most powerful coach in the world: **OURSELVES**.

Remember: You already have the power within yourself to do the things you want to do. You—and only you—can make changes in your life. Sure, I can help you at key points along the way, but I can't wave a magic wand and make you thinner, wealthier, or happier. I don't have the power to earn a promotion for you or close a major sale. The only person who has that power is you. And I don't have a magic wand that can help you, but you do… that magic wand is the instructions you feed your mindset.

You are your own coach now. So, are you ready for your first coaching challenge? Good. Here it comes. You know the old saying, "No one can make you feel bad about yourself without your permission"? It's true. So the big coaching question for today is: Why should you ever give yourself permission to feel miserable?

By the way, the converse is also true. No one can make you feel *good* about yourself without your permission. Which way is it going to go? Which permission will you give?

Imagine that you are a coach and you are coaching someone just like you. Would you tell that person the same things you tell yourself: "You can't do it. Don't even try. You know, this is a waste of time"? Of course you wouldn't! You'd be invested in that person's success and would do and say everything you could to create results!

But still, as our own coaches, we are guilty of sabotaging our own success with our words, thoughts, and beliefs—sometimes even before we begin.

Again, you are in charge here. I can guide you, but ultimately you are the driver on your journey. You have control over your destiny, and no one else can take that control from you without your permission.

If you really want to achieve something, you must believe that you can. That belief has to be stronger than any doubt that might have previously existed. You must be willing to be your own coach, your strongest supporter, and your biggest cheerleader. You must build a relationship based on trust—with yourself. Using the techniques I have shared with you on previous days, I know you can unlock the power within yourself and become your own coach.

THE POWER OF WORDS, REVISITED

Let me remind you at this critical point in the Leverage Your Mindset program that *words are magic to a receptive listener...*and that *you* are the most important listener of all. Yes, it actually is all about *you*.

Here's a story that illustrates the point. Eldrick, a golfer, was slated to be the greatest of all time. His fans and the media were in awe of his skills and had high expectations for him. Just when he was on top of the world, though, personal disaster struck. His divorce was highly publicized, and he didn't just fall from fame—he tumbled hard. Of course, such public scrutiny and personal problems affected his ability to perform at his best. But he wasn't ready to give up and continued to work to overcome his challenges.

Then he suffered another setback, and a personal injury created physical problems that made it difficult to play and to compete. Years went by, and most people believed that his best days were over—he would never play at the champion caliber again. But Eldrick didn't agree. He refused to give up, and he truly believed it was possible to create success once again doing what he loved. Simply put, he developed newfound trust in himself and let that fuel his actions and performance.

By now you might recognize who I'm talking about: Eldrick Tont Woods, better known to the world as Tiger Woods. Tiger overcame significant challenges that would have caused others with less trust and belief in themselves to give up. And he proved just how powerful that trust can be when he won one of America's greatest golf tournaments, the Masters, in 2019 for the fifth time.

Tiger didn't return to fame and victory by telling himself that it was impossible. No, he had to build an unwavering belief and trust in his emotional, mental, and physical ability to become a champion once again.

What you say—and think—always matters. Every single word that crosses your mind, every word you say, and every word you write help frame your personal reality, and, to some extent, the reality about yourself that you present to others around you. If the words are negative, you will find yourself living in a narrow, limited—and probably unhappy—reality. Feeding ourselves negativity only reinforces and cements the likelihood that we'll remain stuck right where we are. It is why the status quo is often perceived negatively. Changing our thoughts and words to positive ones, however, extracts us from our current reality and magnetically propels us toward positive outcomes. If the words you feed yourself are positive, your world expands to virtually limitless horizons.

For example, if you are one of the many people who say, "I can't speak in public," or "I wish I could speak in public," then you've already narrowed the reality of your world and limited what you can accomplish. Incidentally, you've also set yourself up for failure when you are forced to speak in public. But let's suppose you told yourself, "I could learn to speak in public. I have no problem talking to a few people, so I could talk to a few more." Pretty soon, you'd find yourself thinking and saying, "Sure, I can speak in public." And you'll believe it! You're the very same person you were, but now you believe and trust that you are capable of doing something that you'd convinced yourself you couldn't do. That's the power that our thoughts have on our mindset. It's the coach you can take with you everywhere.

The biggest obstacles in front of most of us are the ones we can't see. We can see a mountain and figure out how to go around it or how to climb up it, but sometimes we can't see the obstacles we've spent years building up in our own mind. Increasing your awareness of these obstacles is the key to unlocking the power within and becoming the person you were meant to be.

Today you move beyond "I can't" and "I wish." Today you begin to trust yourself fully...and give yourself permission to live the life you want.

SOFTWARE UPDATES

> A lack of trust harms relationships. Distrust in yourself and your abilities will always negatively impact your results.

> You are the greatest coach in your life. Give yourself the confidence and belief to achieve your goals. Reinforce this trust in your mindset with positive self-talk and imagery, giving it the motivation to succeed.

> Change requires awareness. Become aware of your thoughts and beliefs, and actively replace negative, self-sabotaging thoughts with positive, constructive thoughts and beliefs. You will attempt to accomplish something only if you believe that you can.

❯ Words matter. Feed your mindset with words that support what you want. Make them a daily part of your awareness app and update your thought processes with them.

PROGRESSIVE JUMPS

❯ Take time today to do the following:

- Identify one specific area of your life where you have, up to this point, been saying "I wish." Change that to "I can." Incorporate this new affirmation in your awareness app—and own it.

❯ As a reinforcement tool, you can now listen to "Day Ten" in the audio support program.

REPETITION IS POWER

"Our voice is the center of our expression. Who
we are is spoken by our attitudes, as well
as by the words we choose to say."

TODAY, YOU START getting serious about integrating your awareness app into your routine at multiple points during the day. We are going to focus effort on repetition.

As we repeatedly stamp positive, reaffirming beliefs in our mind, those thoughts become dominant. They overrule the doubts and fears that formerly sculpted our life. Repetition is the key to making those positive thoughts become automatic ones. This is exactly what constructive thoughts have the power to deliver.

SCHOOL DAYS, REVISITED

When we were learning critical concepts in grade school, repetition increased our competencies, helping us to remember and "own" the lessons that had been taught in class. When we were learning how to spell, most of us had to write our weekly spelling words not once, but ten times. Then we were told to use them in a sentence to ensure that we knew the spelling and the meaning of the words. When it came to math, we had to recite the multiplication tables repeatedly: *one times one is one, one times two is two, one times three is three*, and so on. Once we had the ones down, we moved on to the twos…then continued down the line. Sometimes we'd get stuck, and we'd have to say it over and over and over again until we could whip the answer off the top of our heads without thinking about it.

Why do I remind you of this? Because I want you to remember from your own experience what professional athletes and high achievers in all fields know and practice on a regular basis: in order to truly master a specific skill, we have to repeat it in our head, out loud, and on paper until it becomes second nature, as though we'd always known how to do it.

Whatever we repeat to ourselves is stored in our memory, and whenever we need it we can access it without thinking about it. For example, we know that 7 times 3 is 21. It will always be 21, and the only way that can change in our mind is if we repeatedly tell ourselves differently. We would have to override what is stored in our mind with something different in order for us to come up with a different answer.

Repetition is an essential component of this program for the simple reason that repetition builds habit. Anything and everything we do, think, or say often enough becomes second nature to us and becomes part of our world. The first time we do something, thought is required. The first time we got behind the wheel of a car, we had to think about the gas pedal, the brake, the mirrors, and the rules of the road. But after time, those things become second nature, and we hop behind the wheel and drive without thinking about it at all. Imagine what would happen if we could change our internal thoughts and beliefs and eventually make them the dominant part of our thoughts—thoughts that help us achieve our goals and dreams? We can.

Eventually, Michael Jordan made it look like he had been born with a basketball in his hand. But we know he wasn't. The very first time he picked up a basketball, I flat-out guarantee you he didn't play at NBA-superstar caliber. Reaching that level took constant, relentless practice. He repeated the same shot, layup, or free throw over and over and over again in order for the game to look like second nature to him. Once he mastered those shots, he could execute them without even thinking about it. But mastery did not happen without repetition!

But there is another thing to consider. Repetition is far more effective when it is deliberate. The American Psychological Association reports that major improvement or mastery of a task or skill is not likely to be achieved through the simple act of repeating a task, which is known as rote repetition. According to them, intentional practice and repetition are actually necessary before expert level can be achieved.[9] Michael Jordan and other elite athletes who deliberately implement this practice in their daily lives validate this principle.

It takes **repetition** to master any meaningful skill. And it will take repetition for you to master **relaxation**, **trust**, and the other strategies and techniques you have learned in this book. It's a conscious effort that requires time, concentration, and dedication. It requires the same commitment you showed when you drilled yourself on multiplication tables and the same commitment Michael Jordan showed when he practiced his layups.

By the way, did you notice the three words that I bolded in the paragraph you just read? If not, I'll repeat them for you now:

Relaxation

Trust

Repetition

Did you notice that I deliberately and intentionally repeated three steps in the process taught in this book? It is an incredibly simple process. It has only three steps: You've already begun to get your head around the first two. Today, you go back to school… so you can deliberately and intentionally master the third step of the process—repetition. This takes a little effort, just like mastering your multiplication tables did and just like perfecting layups did for professional athletes like Michael Jordan. But the effort is worth it, because repetition is the place where the magic starts to happen.

RELAX

As you may have already noticed, consciously making it a point to relax won't ingrain relaxation into your daily life right away. One or two times is not enough. We must *repeat* our personal routine for relaxation over and over until it is second nature to us. This must be a deliberate act, which is one reason why I strongly encourage you to schedule it into your daily routine.

Just like starting a workout program, practicing layups, or memorizing multiplication tables, relaxation is something we must remind ourselves to do. And it is something we have to be absolutely sure to do multiple times during the day. After we repeat our personal relaxation routine often enough, it will become a part of our daily life. We won't think about it anymore; we will just automatically do it.

Today, you will get a special Progressive Jump about relaxing that takes this into account.

TRUST

Trust is exactly the same. Building trust in ourselves requires constant *conscious* reminders in order to instill the thoughts and suggestions necessary to reinforce our new way of thinking.

Trust needs to be reinforced constantly throughout your day, just as relaxation does. It's like the old story of "The Little Engine That Could." Remember that one? The little train kept climbing up the hill, saying, "I think I can, I think I can, I think I can." Any break in the rhythm and the thought would have caused that train to lose momentum, and it would have struggled, resorting back to "I can't."

Remember, when we say or think "I can't," we are accepting defeat and failure before we even attempt to do something. Self-doubt actually puts you at the starting line of a course where you will fall short or fail, if you even put in any effort at all. Of course you "can't do it"—because that is what you've ingrained into your mindset. And guess what? Your mindset always, *always* works to produce the outcome or results that align with your most dominant thoughts.

The good news is we can change our thoughts to align with what we want! We can be the little train that tells itself what is possible. "I can" is our repeated mantra, too…if we're serious about making trust a reality in our daily lives.

The life we want and deserve is too important for "I can't." If we don't truly believe that we're capable of achieving what we want or becoming who we want to be, we must remind ourselves that we are capable by repeating "I can" and its variations over and over, by enhancing our awareness app continually until the belief in our capability is an automatic response—until it becomes part of who we are.

"The life we want and deserve is too important for "I can't."

As you repeatedly stamp positive, reaffirming beliefs in your mind, they become dominant and overrule the doubts and fears that formerly defined your life. Your mindset is a sponge waiting to absorb whatever you choose to feed it. You can feed it fear... or you can feed it trust. Today, you start feeding it trust multiple times during the day.

REPEAT

Repetition creates a familiar place in your life where positive thoughts are your default setting. It creates a zone of comfort, presence, and readiness.

There is a reason why we say that athletes are "in the zone." They are! They are "mentally" in that place of comfort, presence, and readiness! They create and repeat the thoughts, suggestions, and imagery that they desire. In doing so, they commit themselves to making that desire a reality.

I have worked with collegiate and professional athletes to help them get in the zone for peak performance. In business, it is called being "in the flow." When this happens, confidence is at its highest and we have a laser-like focus. There is complete absorption in the task at hand, and outside distractions don't exist. However, this flow cannot happen without our mindset.

Why is that? Because our mindset cannot be in the zone, or in the flow, unless it feels comfortable with the task. How do you get comfortable with the task? Conscious, deliberate repetition will make the task second nature to you, which is when it is automatic—a very comfortable state. Add trust, and our mindset will go into overdrive to help us achieve the outcome and results that we *know* are possible.

The process of using our thoughts and minds to achieve a flow state is quite effective. A study of golfers and archers revealed that those who practiced mental training were better able to achieve a flow state. The more mental training they did, the higher their ability became to be in the zone, and the better they became at performing without distractions—both distractions around them and internal distractions, such as negative thoughts or feelings.[10]

Professional athletes and highly competitive individuals know that their mind is critical to peak performance. They understand that their thoughts have the ability to determine their outcomes. We don't have to be world champions to implement this principle in our lives. Any thought, visualization, or sound that is repeated in our mind frames the way we think. Whatever we surround ourselves with repeatedly has the power to guide our thoughts, our actions, and our results.

I'm sure you've heard some variation of the expression "Keep saying it and you will start believing it." This is a reliable, time-tested principle, one that really can be counted on to deliver results for you—positive or negative. A great example of this is hearing our parents repeatedly telling us things when we were kids: "Look before you cross the street." "Don't talk to strangers." "Buckle your seat belt." These are just some of the things we've learned from being told something over and over again until we got tired of hearing it. But you know what? These ideas form our outlook and influence our behaviors to this day!

Often, we knew what was coming out of Dad's mouth before he even said it. "Behave yourself and be careful. Be home by 10:00." Sometimes, we'd even mouth it along with him or say, "I know, I know." Then, on our way out the door, we'd adamantly declare that we wouldn't grow up to be like our parents. But when we have our own children, what do we do? We repeat the exact same words that were drilled into our heads when we were kids. They stuck...and the reason they stuck is because they were repeated so often.

This is a good time to remember that our parents did more than admonish us. Often, they were our biggest cheerleaders, yelling from the bleachers, "That's okay, you'll hit it next time!" or "Come on, you can do it!" Maybe those words were what kept us in the game. Maybe they kept us focused and committed to trying. Maybe we say the same things to our own kids today!

It's possible that the encouraging words we received from parents or others when we were doing our homework helped us just as much. "Keep trying; it will come to you." If you're like me, you realize that you also repeat these things to your own kids. Yet so often, when we grow up, we forget to apply those encouraging words to ourselves. Sure, we remember them. We repeat them to our kids and provide the same words of encouragement and support to our friends, siblings, and co-workers when they need a boost. So why do we neglect to tell them to ourselves and, better yet, repeat them until these thoughts come naturally? Until we find ourselves in the zone?

This is what the process of Leverage Your Mindset is all about—repeating, reinforcing, and reexamining; taking care of yourself; and changing your opinions and thoughts to positive, supporting ones so they become second nature. Once they do become second nature, you can finally give yourself the necessary support you've routinely given other important people in your life.

Tell yourself something often enough, and you'll definitely believe it, remember it, and apply it. Practice the three simple principles I have shared with you—relax, trust, and repeat—and consciously and deliberately commit to them every single day, starting today and continuing for the rest of your life. If you can do that, you'll become a master at framing your own reality.

We know the kind of encouragement we're discussing here works. We tell other people to do it all the time. Isn't it about time we remembered to do it for ourselves?

REPEAT UNTIL YOU SHIFT YOUR MINDSET—AND THEN KEEP REPEATING

Repeating what you've learned about relaxation and trust needs to become part of your lifestyle, part of your identity. Why? Because repetition is the single best way to program your mindset for your peak performance and success.

Your mindset doesn't want to let you down. If you repeat something often enough to it, then sure enough, you will believe it, respond to it, and act on it. You will live it. The same, as we have seen, is true in the opposite direction: if you say you *don't* have the potential or the ability to do something, your mind hears that as a valid belief. It works to make that thought a reality.

Whether you're a salesperson continuing to grow your network and provide solutions to clients, or a leader striving to gain the full focus and participation of your team, or even an athlete striving to improve your mental awareness of your ability and potential, you can be in the zone, functioning at peak performance, if you want to—and if you believe you can. *Your reality is based on what you believe, and what you believe is based on what you repeat.* So make sure you're repeating the right stuff!

SOFTWARE UPDATES

> Success through this program is a three-step process: relax, trust, and repeat. Together with positive thoughts, these three steps, when performed intentionally, consciously, and repeatedly, will lead to increased success in achieving your goals and getting the most out of your life.

> Repetition is the conscious and deliberate practice that is necessary for success. Repetition is crucial for implementing your awareness app so it becomes second nature and operates without conscious thought.

> Being in the zone or in the flow means that you are intently focused and functioning at peak performance. Anyone can achieve this state through the steps taught in this book: relaxation, trust, and the repetition of positive self-talk and mental imagery.

PROGRESSIVE JUMPS

> Take some time during the day to relax and review your awareness app in a fully trusting mindset. Conduct this update in a private area where you will not be distracted.

> As a reinforcement tool, you can now listen to "Day Eleven" in the audio support program.

DAY TWELVE

THE MINDSET MAGNET™

"Don't let memories of the past or concerns
about the future hold back the power
of living in the present."

TODAY IS ALL ABOUT your Mindset Magnet. A Mindset Magnet is a compass that constantly points you toward your best self and your best outcomes, no matter what happens. It's what ensures that your mental app is working to maximize your greatest asset—yourself—so that you can live your best life.

Using a Mindset Magnet is not just a one-time event. It is a specific way of living over time—an outlook that *automatically* draws what you want to be, have, and do closer to you, minute after minute, hour after hour, day after day. Every truly successful person has a Mindset Magnet that attracts and manifests their desires, and you can, too.

All it takes to create a Mindset Magnet is three easy, yet extremely effective, principles. Those principles are the same ones that we've been reiterating throughout this book: relax, trust, and repeat. You've already put them into practice, and now it's time to truly master them. The nine insights I will be sharing with you in this chapter will position you to do exactly that.

RELAXATION: THREE INSIGHTS TO MAGNETIZE YOUR MINDSET

ONE: It's helpful to focus on why you're relaxing. You're relaxing to reduce stress and clear your mind of the distractions and constant disruptions that prevent you from giving 100 percent of your focus and attention. This gives your mind a clean slate, devoid of negative thoughts, anxiety, stress, and interruptions. When your mind is in this state of relaxation, your mindset is more accessible and accepting of the constructive thoughts and suggestions that you feed it.

You now know that your mindset is an invaluable asset with unlimited possibilities. It is infinite. It has no boundaries. There are no limits to its capacity. It can function on what is already there, without requiring further nourishment or attention, or it can continually be exercised and fed with new thoughts, suggestions, emotions, and experiences. But in order to gain access to it and make it a consistent positive force in your life, you need to make relaxation part of your daily lifestyle! Think of relaxation as the ticket you need to access the incomprehensible power of your mindset. You can't tap into this power unless you make relaxation a part of your daily routine. That is why it is so important to make it a daily habit to step back and take deep breaths at multiple points during your day. It's a prerequisite for tapping into the power of your mindset…and exceeding your own expectations.

TWO: You can always choose to breathe consciously. The best and simplest way to relax in an instant, even when you think you don't have time for it, is to take two or three nice, long, deep breaths. This is a life skill—and a survival skill. Doing this is a great way to slow everything down, and I find that it's also a great way to build a foundation of gratitude in my life. Whenever I take a deep breath—and I mean a really deep breath, one that's conscious in both the inhale and the exhale—I am more present in the moment. I perceive myself to be more fortunate, and I attract more fortune into my life, whether it's friendship, financial success, or any other example of "fortune." By taking a big deep breath and slowly letting it go, I always find my way back to the gift of living more fully in the present. I think about the specific blessings in my life. For instance: "Today I can be grateful that I have the opportunity and the gift of a breath of life-giving air. I'm alive, not dead. I'm so grateful for that." That's pretty blunt, but it's true. When I appreciate that deep breath of air and become aware of it, I am presented with an opportunity to take another breath. And I relax. You can do the same—any time you choose. Remember: Whenever we're relaxed enough to be grateful for the positive things in our life, we attract more of those things. Whenever we're tense and ungrateful, we tend to dwell on the negative and, therefore, invite more of the negative into our life. Breathing deeply, in gratitude, is an indispensable component of true success. When you breathe deeply and let the breath go back out slowly, you relax your whole body. Do that throughout the day!

THREE: Rest is not the same thing as relaxation. Ask yourself a tough question. You've been doing this for 11 days now. It's time for a reality check. Have you made it a positive habit to sit down and take some time for the sole purpose of giving yourself the devoted attention and awareness you need to relax, focus, and affirm your goals? I'm hoping the answer is yes, because that is required for you to benefit from this program. A lot of people think that sitting down for 15 minutes to read the paper or watch YouTube videos is relaxation. It may be an enjoyable part of your day, but for the purposes of building your Mindset Magnet, we know that's not relaxation. As a matter of fact, a study conducted by Johannes Gutenberg University Mainz in Germany and VU University Amsterdam found that when people watched television or videos after a stressful day at work, it didn't result in personal recovery or recharging. On the contrary, it made people feel like they had less control, and they became frustrated and depressed.[11]

When I say "relaxation," I'm referring to time spent with only your thoughts and the intention to relax, without a book, television shows, computer screens, phones, or worries about yesterday and tomorrow. This program requires you to reclaim that kind of personal time! The ability to relax and empty your mind and body of the constant chatter is vital to activating your Mindset Magnet. You can deliver instructions to your mindset only when you have entered a place where you are truly relaxed, focused, and able to affirm your thoughts. When your mindset stops judging and limiting your thinking, you are able to remove all distractions and reprogram your state of mind in a way that makes sense to you, based on what you want to achieve and the person you choose to become.

TRUST: THREE INSIGHTS TO MAGNETIZE YOUR LIFE

ONE: Trust is about moving forward in life. Trust is the key to discovering the person you were meant to be. It is the commitment to give yourself permission to live life at your full potential…and perhaps to realize that this kind of life is a direction, not a destination; a way to be more accountable and responsible to yourself and to other people. You can call this commitment by any name you want: faith in yourself, faith in a Higher Power, certainty, purpose, whatever. The title you give it is immaterial. What matters is that you use that force to harness your natural capacity to learn, grow, challenge your comfort zones, and move forward in life. Martin Luther King Jr. once gave a marvelous definition of faith, one that perfectly captures what I mean when I say "trust." He said, "Faith is taking the first step even when you don't see the whole staircase. Take the first step in faith. You don't have to see the whole staircase. Just take the first step."

TWO: Trust means consciously harnessing the power of words—for your own benefit. Suppose that you were interviewing someone for an important position and during your discussion that person spoke poorly of himself. The words he chose dismissed his potential and focused on his past failures, expressing low self-esteem and negativity, as opposed to his possibilities, goals, and the things he was committed to doing. Would you hire this person? Probably not, because a lack of trust in ourselves is transferred to others.

The words we use, especially in reference to ourselves, always matter. Doctors have found that it only takes one negative word to activate the amygdala, which is the part of the brain that produces and responds to fear. Once activated, the amygdala releases hormones and neurotransmitters that produce stress and disrupt the brain's ability to focus and function at its full potential.[12]

If you interview people and want them to speak to you with confidence and the belief that they're capable, qualified, and an asset to your team, shouldn't you be holding yourself to the same standard? Whatever you are doing, whatever your grand design is, whatever your products or services are, and wherever you are headed in life, when you speak to yourself with full confidence and competence, choosing words that make it easier for you to trust your best instincts, you are in the driver's seat. Recognize that it is the words you choose to feed to your mindset and the actions you take in response to those words that will make you happy, sad, excited, bored, interested, committed, successful, or unsuccessful. Those words will determine if you help or hinder the results you want to achieve. If you really want to commit to yourself and bettering your life, feed your mindset a steady stream of positive words and phrases. What do you love? What are you good at? What are you excited about? What are you committed to? What are you achieving, right now?

THREE: Trust is either increasing or decreasing. It is never static. Do you remember that old Bob Dylan lyric, "He who is not busy being born is busy dying"? I've got a little secret for you: that's really all about the level of trust you have in yourself and your purpose here on earth. You're never in a neutral position. You're either moving toward your life's best possible expression or you're moving away from it. That's just the way life works. So get busy being born!

REPETITION: THREE INSIGHTS TO MAGNETIZE YOUR LIFE

ONE: Internal repetition determines external results. Remember, the thoughts you repeat in your mind determine your results—not the circumstances you encounter in life. What kinds of messages will you choose to repeat internally? Will they be constructive or destructive thoughts? If it's something like "Can I really lose weight?" you're going to create an external outcome that matches that repetition. The destructive thoughts may say, "Not today. It's too hard. I could never have that much willpower." But what if you chose to repeat one or more of the following constructive thoughts: "I am losing weight"; "I am eating healthier today"; "I am noticing what I choose to eat and making decisions that support me"; "My level of physical activity is high and getting higher"; "My willpower is strong"? When you put those kinds of thoughts into your awareness app and repeat them, your mindset hears them, believes them, and looks for opportunities to create the outcomes you are envisioning.

TWO: Repeated constructive internal thoughts repel negativity and attract positive resources for you and everyone in your circle. Being able to use constructive thoughts repetitively so that they become AutoThoughts is the winning characteristic, the key lifestyle trait, that attracts not only a positive outcome for you in your life, but also for those with whom you interact. A rising tide lifts all boats! A sustained effort to make constructive thoughts a natural part of who you are raises the level of possibility and achievement, not only in your own life, but in all of your important relationships.

This is a particularly vital concept for people who are using this system to lead teams and create better business relationships. When you repel negativity with affirmations like "I provide my clients with the best solutions" or "I give the members of my team the support they need," you are finding ways to add value to the lives of those who are lucky enough to work with you!

THREE: Repeated constructive thoughts that are rooted in intention allow you to take full control of your life. There are two ways to build constructive thoughts into your life: randomly and intentionally. Obviously, random thoughts are just that—random. They are spontaneous and are triggered by other people, events, or situations. At times, random positive thoughts—the ones you happen to feed your mindset without intentionally writing them into your awareness app—do have good outcomes. I don't mean to minimize them. They are valuable and can spark the implementation of an idea…but more often than not, they are not connected to any long-term desire, plan, or purpose.

The planned, intentional repetition of your own most motivating positive thoughts, however, is a far more powerful event. When the mind is relaxed and focused on a thought that you have chosen carefully, one that is designed to match up with your goals and that you have chosen to feed into your mindset over and over again, something remarkable happens. Your mindset chooses to engrave that thought into your belief system, your sense of "what the world is." That consciously chosen thought then spreads, strengthens, and dominates your mind, creating a greater sense of purpose and control in your experience of life, no matter what obstacles you may encounter. Over time, these intentional thoughts replace former destructive AutoThoughts, and they become a habit—you believe them and embed that belief in everything you do. They become second nature and part of who you are and how you act.

Clarity from relaxation and trust, combined with steady repetition of a powerful constructive thought like "I am unstoppable," builds faith and belief in that chosen thought—and eventually makes the thought your guiding daily reality. It becomes a constructive AutoThought—an anchor in your world, something to which you can return any time you need to remind yourself of who's really in charge of your journey through life.

SOFTWARE UPDATES

> Your mindset is a magnet that can actually bring you closer to what you want to accomplish, become, or have.

> Reinforce the three simple, but very effective, principles to create a Mindset Magnet: relax, trust, and repeat.

> Destructive words can activate the fear center of the brain and cause it to release stress-producing hormones. Replace them with intentional constructive thoughts that support and reinforce what you want.

> Repetition will turn a former destructive belief or habit into a powerful constructive belief or habit.

PROGRESSIVE JUMPS

> In addition to listening to the audio program and doing your normal relaxation activities today, I want you to:

- Envision that you are a Mindset Magnet. Visualize being in a relaxed state where you are automatically drawn to and guided toward what you want. Do this in a very quiet area where there are no distractions and you can remain fully focused on what you want.

- Continue the pattern of taking some time to review your awareness app in a fully trusting mindset. Double-check your subconscious grocery list and make sure you're repeating the affirmations you need to be progressing toward what you want.

- Take a few minutes to identify your internal thoughts. Are they constructive or destructive? Rewrite any destructive, self-sabotaging thoughts as positive affirmations. Make it a part of your daily routine to relax and focus on repeating those affirmations and trusting that you can achieve them.

> As a reinforcement tool, you can now listen to "Day Twelve" in the audio support program.

HOW TO FEEL AMAZING

"You always have the power to change your thought process from doubt, disbelief, or frustration to possibility and peak performance."

ONE SIMPLE THOUGHT

IT'S AMAZING HOW the human mind can either restrict our success or enhance it. The key word here is *amazing*. I chose it for a reason.

Just one simple thought or belief can reveal, transform, and inspire your mind. What if that one simple thought or belief literally made you amazing?

Consciously and unconsciously communicating the simple repeated message "I feel amazing" is one of the most powerful things you can do to activate your Mindset Magnet. Today, that's what you're going to learn how to do. I think you'll find that the simple strategy I'm going to share with you today is an instant game changer. It's what you've been building up to for the last 12 days.

Feeling amazing is what makes you amazing. So make the most of this game changer…and be sure to read and carefully follow the instructions you'll be getting at the end of this chapter.

LET ME ASK YOU A QUESTION...

Do you want to exceed your own expectations…or are you comfortable staying where you are in terms of your present position, status, financial goals, and wellness?

By this point in our time together, I am hoping that the answer to that question was immediate and instinctive. I am hoping that by now, you are deeply committed to exceeding your own expectations in each of these areas.

If you are, I have good news for you: you now have the capability to instantly create a different reality, a transformative reality, in *all* aspects of your life. Thanks to all the work you have done on Days 1 through 12, you now have access to all the tools you need to launch and sustain the state of mind and emotion that will allow you to instantly set in motion a series of actions that will amaze you…when you step back and realize that the results came from you.

Let's start that process.

What I'm about to share with you is the exact opposite of the process you have experienced when attempting to do something while entertaining the underlying belief that it wouldn't work. Then, when it didn't work, you said to yourself, "I knew it wouldn't work." You told others, "I'm not surprised. I knew it wouldn't work."

You were absolutely right. It wasn't going to work. You sabotaged your success with your negative beliefs. By the way, the word *sabotage* derives from the action of workers throwing their wooden shoes, called *sabots*, into machinery in an attempt to intentionally destroy it, diminishing their ability to perform their jobs. As it turns out, people today do basically the same thing. They allow negative thoughts and beliefs to sabotage their goals. For instance, believing they can never meet, much less exceed, a sales goal, they don't even try. They just throw their shoes into the metaphorical machine.

Here's what that sabotage sounds like:

"I wish I had a territory as good as Jane's."

"I could never be as good at delivering presentations as Tom is."

"Decision makers don't want to talk to me."

That's the sound of someone throwing shoes into the machinery. Today, for you, that self-sabotage stops.

"Today, for you, that self-sabotage stops.

Whether you want to accomplish professional goals, reduce stress at work or at home, improve your health and wellness, or overcome bad habits, you now know that you can. You now have direct experience in replacing negativity and doubts with powerful positive beliefs. As a result, there is no limit to what you can accomplish—if you are willing to assume personal responsibility for managing your own mental and emotional states. Once you make that commitment, you realize that you are the only person in control of your success—and the only person who ever could be.

Studies have proven that our mind has an infinite amount of control over everything we feel, do, and accomplish. In fact, it is the mind, not the body, that has the most control over things like achieving our maximum physical strength and managing pain.

A study conducted by Duke University shows us just how much control the mind has over our bodies and our results. The participants were all given identical pain-reducing placebos. One half of the group were told the medication cost $2.50 per dose. The other half were told the cost was just 10 cents per dose.

Each patient was then administered electric shock via light. The results were fascinating. None of the participants actually received a painkiller—remember, they were given placebos. A remarkable 85 percent of the group that was told their "pain killer" cost $2.50 said it reduced their pain. What about the 50 percent who took the less expensive placebo? Only 61 percent believed it had an effect at all on their pain level.[13]

The study concluded that not only was the mind tricked into believing that a placebo was an effective pain reducer, but our beliefs actually affect our outcomes. In this study, they proved that the perception that more expensive things are better than cheaper alternatives actually impacts our opinion about them and the way we believe they perform.

In truth, there wasn't even one participant who actually received a painkiller at all! The mind (including our belief system) is a remarkable engineer of our reality and outcomes!

So are you ready to leverage that power?

Good.

THE REMOTE CONTROL, REVISITED

We've been working together for nearly two weeks now. If you've been keeping track and following this program up to this point, you now know that you don't have to throw your shoes into the machine. You know that choice is completely up to you.

Recall that right now, in this moment, as you read these words, you still have access to the remote control that will change your thought process from doubt, disbelief, or frustration to *amazing…* at any moment. Working this remote control, you'll remember, is just as easy as changing the channel on your television set. So let's revisit that. We'll do an abbreviated version of the remote control process right now, and then an in-depth version of it using the track "Day Thirteen" in the audio program once you have finished this chapter. Ready?

I want you to take three deep breaths before you read the next paragraph. Exhale each breath out slowly. Did you do that? Did you RELAX with three deep inhales and three slow exhales? Good.

Now I want you to think of a very happy, memorable moment of your life. It can be anything—an occasion, an accomplishment, a celebration—as long as it naturally makes you smile. It might be a professional or personal accomplishment. I don't know what it is for you. The moment is different for everyone. You have to find the right moment for you. What comes to mind that makes you smile?

Don't just choose any pleasant memory. Choose something that literally makes you smile the instant you visualize this event. Got it? If not, stop here and wait until that moment comes to mind and you are smiling. If you are thinking of this special moment, and you are smiling right now, and you are experiencing full TRUST in your right to re-occupy and re-experience that moment any time you choose, please continue to the next page.

Welcome back. You're now thinking about this positive memory, picturing it, hearing it, and you're smiling. You're feeling the powerful positive emotion that you experienced as a result of having been alive and present in that special moment. What I want you to notice right now is how your perspective has changed.

Whatever was going on before you focused with full attention and full presence on that memory is now irrelevant. You have the remote control in your hand. You have pressed the button. You have changed the experience, the outlook, and the perspective to one of happiness. Feel gratitude for having experienced a moment like that. Feel gratitude for the ability to notice and re-experience that moment...*whenever* you want.

Now get a blank sheet paper and a pen or pencil and write down these words:

I FEEL AMAZING.

Once you have done that, and not before, go on to the next page. Please be absolutely sure that you don't move on to the next page until you have written down these three powerful words using that ancient, analog technology: a writing instrument of some kind.

Don't type them into your phone or a document on your computer. Write them down, letter by letter and word by word, on a physical piece of paper or a sticky note. Then move on to the next page.

If you've followed my instructions carefully, you are now in a happy state of mind and emotion, and you are looking at a sheet of paper with the words "I FEEL AMAZING" written in your own handwriting.

What I want you to do now is to REPEAT those words out loud three times, with increasing intensity and belief each time. Go ahead and do that right now.

How do you feel?

Amazing, right?

I have a friend who implemented this strategy while fighting cancer. She had 26 weeks of chemotherapy, the first 14 of which she was given the strongest drug available for her disease. The nurses called this drug "the red devil." Now, my friend was given a mini college course informing her of the side effects of her treatment. She was prepared to lose her hair…and weight. She was prepared to be not just tired, but exhausted all the time. She was told not to make plans ahead of time but always to wait and see whether she felt up to it. They heavily prepared her for the reality that there would be good days, but there would be a hefty share of bad days. Knowing all that, an expectation of feeling ill, even miserable, wouldn't be unreasonable. But something different happened. She fought it—but not in the way most people would think. Actually, she used relaxation, constructive thoughts, trust, and repetition to influence her outcome. Before chemotherapy, she sat quietly and relaxed. Breathing in and out, she repeated one saying to herself, "Today is a good day for a good day." The next day, when they told her she was likely to be most ill, she repeated the very same steps. She did this for 26 weeks…and although she did experience fatigue, the strong chemotherapy treatments never made her physically ill.

Our mindset and the beliefs we feed it have an amazing influence on how we feel and react. When we say, "I feel amazing," we really do improve the way we physically and emotionally feel. When we say, "Today is a good day for a good day," we really do align our beliefs and our mind to work together to create that reality.

That's some pretty impressive technology. That's the remote control you can operate at any time when you feel yourself picking up a shoe and you're tempted to toss it into the machinery of your mindset, which is waiting for you to activate it to create a deeper level of success and fulfillment in any area of your life. What did you do when you used self-talk and mental imagery to activate a positive memory and then affirmed how amazing you feel?

You RELAXED.

You TRUSTED your right to re-enter and re-experience that moment of profound happiness.

You REPEATED a particularly powerful affirmation, "I FEEL AMAZING," until you reached a stage of experiential belief.

By using those three simple steps, you changed your world. Those three simple steps—RELAX, TRUST, and REPEAT—are the keys to the kingdom. They are your remote control. Use them!

And if you're looking for an abbreviated version of the same process that is almost as powerful, try this: the next time someone asks you how you are doing, smile, look them right in the eye, and say, "Amazing!" or whatever variation works for you. When someone asks me how I am, I like to say, "Fantastic!" The person is usually a bit shocked, and I get a look of wonder and curiosity in response. I like that outcome. I can tell that at some level, they want to know why and how they can be fantastic, too. Isn't this a powerful way to start a conversation? Do you think when someone says, "How are you?" that person really wants to hear about the terrible thing that just happened to you or have you respond with a list of all the things you are busy with? Of course not. Usually "How are you?" is just a good way to start a conversation. Why not start it with a word that makes both people smile—and makes the other person want to know more?

This is just one example, but you get the idea. You always have the remote control that can change the channel, that can reorient your mind to make yourself more *amazing*—more motivated, more grateful, and more successful.

Note that the process always begins with clearing your mind, consciously creating a clean slate so you can begin to rewrite your mental programming, your awareness app. Program your mindset to respond in a way that *supports you*. Clear your mind of your preprogrammed beliefs, stress, and the constant chatter that disrupt your focus. This is how you become the commander in chief of your own life.

As we head into the final days of this program, I challenge you to exceed your own expectations. Through the lifelong journey of self-discovery that you're now ready to undertake, I challenge you to unlock your full potential. I challenge you to stick with it, even after you complete this book. What we are talking about here is really a continual growing process—a way of life—but I can promise you that you'll begin to see positive results quickly... if you will invest the minimal time and effort necessary to send your mindset the daily messages it needs to support you.

It's been said that the power to move the world lies in one's mindset. I believe that with every fiber of my being. In my personal experience, I have witnessed time and time again how any situation—even a potentially difficult one—can be reframed into an I FEEL AMAZING moment. Once I learned how to do that, I learned how to move my own world. I discovered that I did not have to remain tuned in to negative or limiting messages. Instead, I could simply take the remote control and change the channel. By updating your awareness app, you can experience the same awesome power in moving your own world.

The power of suggestion really is the key to leveraging the enormous untapped potential of your mindset. I have now shared with you the secrets of mastering the art of personal suggestion to activate your personal Mindset Magnet. Use what I have shared with you over the past 13 days to allow your mindset to frame a new reality, one that supports the person you were meant to become—the best possible version of yourself, with the most success and the most fulfillment. Using relaxation techniques, full trust, and the power of repetition, you can now leverage the power of suggestion to create, and act on, opportunities for change and growth that will vastly exceed your own expectations.

You're about to enter your second reinforcement session. After that comes the Epilogue, which contains a special message for you to read once you've completed the final step of this program.

See you tomorrow!

SOFTWARE UPDATES

> Our mindset can either enhance our success or sabotage it.

> The mind and the thoughts we feed it have an amazing ability to impact our outcomes, even our health!

> Whenever you are experiencing negativity, anxiety, stress, etc., you can always change the channel by relaxing and thinking of a happy memory. Pick up the remote control and counter destructive AutoThoughts by turning the channel and watching a rerun of a time when you felt amazing!

> When you think you feel good, you will feel better. When you think you feel amazing, you will feel just that…amazing! So write it down, and say it out loud: "I FEEL AMAZING!"

PROGRESSIVE JUMPS

> By now you should be a pro at taking personal time to clear, calm, and awaken your mindset. This should have

been part of your daily routine. Now it's time to strengthen and reinforce that daily relaxation with specific updates to your awareness app. This is key to reinforcing your personalized constructive AutoThoughts and creating a Mindset Magnet. Please note that this is a very important track! Accordingly, the relaxation exercise will be slightly longer, because now you're going beyond relaxation and reflection and using your updated mental software to actively pursue your goals and become the version of yourself you most want to be. Take full advantage of this relaxation meditation exercise to update your internal hard drive—your awareness app. You have already created a list of the thoughts, beliefs, and accomplishments that you want in life, thereby enhancing your awareness through the act of writing. Everything that you have been practicing up to this point has prepared you to firmly etch this script—your Subconscious Grocery List, as I've termed it—into your subconscious using visualization and affirmation, your Mind's Eye and your Inner Voice. When you reprogram your mindset with this script, your updated awareness app will constantly run in the background, replacing doubt with belief and equipping you with the confidence necessary to create the life you desire. Leaders will find the self-assurance they need to guide their teams with intentionality. Sales professionals will discover the purpose and conviction they need to approach opportunities with boldness.

Those looking to be more consistent with their exercise routines will find that their workouts become less of a grind and instead become a firmly entrenched habit. The applications are endless: whatever you desire, you can reset your path and perspective so that you are progressively moving toward actualizing your goals. So during this relaxation exercise, make sure to visualize your Subconscious Grocery List and rehearse it in your mind using your Inner Voice. As you do, you will not only become more aware of your positive intentions, but you will find that automatically, without even thinking about it, you will regularly act on the items on your list, even when you aren't conscious of it.

> As a reinforcement tool, you can now listen to "Day Thirteen" in the audio support program.

IT'S ALREADY STARTED

"By becoming aware of the boundaries we
place on ourselves, we can learn how
to push beyond them."

BEFORE YOU STARTED this life-changing 14-day program, your mindset was already guiding you and shaping your perceptions, your world, and your outcomes. You were already sending your mindset messages about what you expected from life, and your mindset was dutifully carrying out those instructions and creating that world for you. You were already choosing the words you used in your internal monologue, and those words either took you closer or further away from actualizing your goals and dreams. The only new variable in your situation is that you've now begun a new phase of the process...by simply becoming aware of what you most want to create in your life and discovering that you have the ability to make it happen.

As you put everything you've learned thus far into practice, I challenge you to harness the power of awareness.

The minute you become aware, things start to happen. Awareness that you wanted to enhance your skills or create positive change in your life is what caused you to read this book. Awareness of what you are truly capable of—what you aspire to do, become, or achieve—is what will keep you moving forward today and in all the days to come. Just by creating awareness that you want to accomplish something specific, you've started the ball rolling. You've put a thought or a suggestion in your mind. Your mind will now use that thought or suggestion to help you make it your reality. Again, it's already happening. The key that will ignite the engine of your life is *awareness*.

This program is like many other things in life. Leverage Your Mindset requires attention, practice, and repetition in order to deliver the maximum benefit. The more you focus on it, the more powerful it will be. This process has already been in place regardless of whether you've been conscious of it and whether you've been using it to help or to hurt you. The beauty of this system is that it allows *you* to direct the process. It puts you—not luck, circumstances, or anything else—in control. What you will do today—and every day thereafter—is take control of the process by means of heightened awareness.

To create a deeper level of awareness, I'd like you to ask and honestly answer these questions, using your phone, a notebook, or a document on your computer:

> ❯ What do I really want? What do I most want to change in my life?

> ❯ How will I know for sure when this has happened?

> What will it look like, sound like, and feel like for me as I experience this?

> What is my time frame for accomplishing this? What is my plan?

Please give yourself at least five minutes of writing time to address each of these four issues. This is your critical reinforcement activity. Don't skip it!

Use this activity to gain clarity and awareness. Be as specific as possible.

Leverage Your Mindset is the first step toward all accomplishments in personal and professional development. Knowing what you want is necessary before you can go out and get it. Then, hold yourself accountable. Make a personal commitment to take action toward that goal. Awareness needs to team up with action to produce results. No one can do it for you. This is your dream, your desire, your future…and you have the tools you need to make it happen.

"In your mindset, all things are possible.

As you move forward, follow the relaxation, breathing, and awareness app techniques you have learned here. Do them every day. The more you practice them, the more effective they'll become. The awareness of who you really are, what you are truly capable of, and what your next step is will become more dominant in your mindset once you're relaxed and have a clear mind. Then—take action!

Your awareness app is always running. You cannot turn it off. However, it takes time for your new thoughts and beliefs to become more prominent than the former destructive thoughts and beliefs that were written into your mindset. That is why you have to make it a daily practice to enhance your awareness. Your new constructive thoughts will not become automatic, running constantly in the program that guides your results and your life, until they become a habitual way of thinking. It's your responsibility to take the thoughts and suggestions and nurture them, minute by minute and day by day. Once you make that a habit, you'll begin to see progress as you become less stressed, more driven and passionate about your best aspirations, and more invested in supporting your own growth and development.

It's up to you: your mindset can be your worst enemy or your best friend. The choices you make will determine which of those two outcomes you experience. I've witnessed the transformation thousands of times as I watched clients change their habits, focus on their goals, and become the people they were meant to be.

Yes, it's already started. Your journey began before you even picked up this book. It will continue after you've finished reading the final page. The only question is whether you will be setting the course. The real key to creating change and achieving goals lies, not in the world outside, but within your mindset. In your mindset, all things are possible.

Change the way you think, and you will change your world!

SOFTWARE UPDATES

> Your mindset has always been working to align your results with your deepest beliefs and thoughts. If you believe what you want is not possible, your mindset will go to work to prove that you're right. However, if you feed your mindset positive, constructive thoughts that support the outcome you really do want, your mindset will magnetize you toward it.

> Leverage Your Mindset is the key to maximizing your most valuable asset—yourself. You must know what you want, who you want to be, the things you want to accomplish, etc., before your awareness app can run the program that will deliver those results.

> This is a 14-day program, but the longer and more consistently you implement it, including completing the exercises in this book, the more efficient and effective it becomes. Make it part of your everyday routine so that it becomes second nature and you find yourself implementing it in your life without even thinking about it. It is a small change in your daily routine that will create monumental transformations in every area of your life.

PROGRESSIVE JUMPS

> ACT every day! Air—Intentional Breathing, Change Your Imagery, and Take Time to Recharge!

> Use your relaxation meditation exercise to update your awareness app. You have already written a list of the thoughts, beliefs, and accomplishments that you want in life—your Subconscious Grocery List. Make updating your internal hard drive with this list part of your daily routine, and continue to perform updates to your mindset—your awareness app—after you have finished this book. Create space for this in your schedule for the 14 days following tomorrow, and repeat the process every 14 days thereafter. This continual updating of your awareness app will ensure that your mindset is programmed to keep you moving, both consciously and unconsciously, toward the decisions, actions, and results you desire. It will keep you on autopilot toward becoming the version of yourself you truly want to be. Remember, your potential is not an end point; it is an ever-expanding horizon. Better is possible—you simply need to leverage your mindset to make it work for, rather than against, you.

> Make RELAX, TRUST, and REPEAT part of your daily operating plan.

> As a reinforcement tool, you can now listen to "Day Fourteen" in the audio support program.

IT'S YOUR CHOICE

I HAVE A FEW THOUGHTS to share with you before we part. First, do not take the steps in this program for granted. I know from personal experience that they work, as they have helped me through some challenging times. I have also witnessed the life-changing effects they've had for the thousands of people I have helped over the years. If it can do that for so many people, I know that it can help you make a positive change, too.

Second, don't let the conclusion of this program serve as an end point on your journey toward personal growth and fulfillment. Just like your computer requires periodic updates, maintenance, and other care, so will your mindset require a continual investment of time, attention, and awareness. Remember, you are your most valuable asset. There is no one on this earth quite like you, and you cannot maximize your value if you're running on outdated software. The stakes are too large to drop the ball here. You now know what it's like to feel amazing—to feel calm, grateful, focused, capable, and motivated. Don't let these feelings be fleeting. You absolutely can experience these emotions consistently IF you leverage the power of your mindset. Even on your worst days, recognize that the world is not coming down on you. The constructive AutoThoughts you develop in and beyond this program can help you reframe obstacles and temporary challenges as opportunities for growth. Every problem and difficulty that you face, if viewed correctly, is an invitation to expand your possibilities and broaden your frame of reference. If you feel those destructive AutoThoughts creeping back in, remember to return to the basics: RELAX, TRUST, and REPEAT. Magnetize your mindset and recalibrate your awareness app so that it's functioning in the direction of what you want in life, not what threatens to take that away.

The third message is equally simple and equally powerful: I want you to find your guiding purpose in life…and make sure that whatever you are pursuing next matches up with it. Success means different things for different people. For some, this program will help them reduce their stress levels and find more presence in the moment. For others, it will provide a level of awareness and intentionality that will bring them professional success and financial prosperity. Still yet, others will find that it helps them strengthen interpersonal relationships, become better leaders, increase their health and well-being, or simply improve their overall drive and focus. You have complete control over the results this program can bring you: only you can identify what it means to be the best version of yourself; what specific goals you can achieve to live a happier, more meaningful life; and what steps you need to take to translate your mindset into actionable results.

I hope this book created that awareness within you and the desire to discover your purpose and what you really want in life. You have invested 14 days into this process and are on your way to making the maintenance of your awareness app a positive habit that will always, always work for you. Again, don't stop now! It would be like stopping a weight-loss program that is working before you've reached your goal. This is not a 14-day change; it's a lifestyle change—one that transforms your perceptions, your expectations, and your outcomes. Be persistent with this program, remain committed, and you will continue to experience positive results. Each time you repeat the program, you will discover that your potential is not an end point but a moving target on an ever-broadening horizon.

You already have everything you need to achieve your goals and create the life you want. Your mindset is ready and waiting to work with you. It is the internal GPS that knows the fastest route to success is through your thoughts.

Isn't it finally time for you to leverage your most important asset—you?

Choose to be optimistic!

Choose to lead from within!

Choose to be remarkable!

Choose to be BOLD!

Choose to change the way you think, and you will change your world!

PROGRESSIVE JUMP

> As you conclude this book, please listen to the final track of the audio support program.

NOTES

1. Sara Reistad-Long, "Positive Thinking Sets You Up for Success," *WebMD*, http://www.webmd.com/balance/features/power -positive-thinking#1.

2. Barbara L. Fredrickson, "The Broaden-and-Build Theory of Positive Emotions," *Philosophical Transactions of the Royal Society B* 359, no. 1449 (September 29, 2004): 1367–78. http://www.ncbi.nlm.nih.gov/pmc/articles/PMC1693418/ pdf/15347528.pdf.

3. W. Staffen, et al., "Selective Brain Activity in Response to One's Own Name in the Persistent Vegetative State," *Journal of Neurology, Neurosurgery & Psychiatry* 77, no. 12 (December 2006): 1383–84. http://www.ncbi.nlm.nih.gov/pmc/articles/ PMC2077408/#.

4. Joel Wong and Joshua A. Brown, "How Gratitude Changes You and Your Brain," *Greater Good Magazine*, June 6, 2017, http:// greatergood.berkeley.edu/article/item/how_gratitude_changes _you_and_your_brain.

5. "Study Focuses on Strategies for Achieving Goals, Resolutions," *Dominican University of California*, http://www.dominican.edu/dominicannews/study-highlights-strategies-for-achieving-goals.

6. Lyubomirsky, S., King, L., and Diener, E. "The Benefits of Frequent Positive Affect: Does Happiness Lead to Success?" *Psychological Bulletin* 131, no. 6 (2005): 803–55.

7. Gail Matthews, "Goals Research Summary," *Dominican University of California*, http://www.dominican.edu/academics/lae/undergraduate-programs/psych/faculty/assets-gail-matthews/researchsummary2.pdf.

8. Bryan Borzykowski, "Why Talking to Yourself Is the First Sign of Success," *BBC.com*, April 27, 2017, http://www.bbc.com/worklife/article/20170428-why-talking-to-yourself-is-the-first-sign-of-success.

9. Mary Brabeck, Jill Jeffrey, and Sara Fry, "Practice for Knowledge Acquisition (Not Drill and Kill)," *American Psychological Association*, http://www.apa.org/education/k12/practice-acquisition.

10. K. A. Kaufman, C. R. Glass, and D. B. Arnkoff, "Evaluation of Mindful Sport Performance Enhancement (MSPE): A New Approach to Promote Flow in Athletes." *Journal of Clinical Sport Psychology* 4 (2009): 334–56.

11. Leonard Reinecke and Wilhelm Hofmann, "Slacking Off or Winding Down? An Experience Sampling Study on the Drivers and Consequences of Media Use for Recovery Versus Procrastination," *Human Communication Research* 42, no. 3 (2016): 441–61.

12. Therese J. Bouchard, "Words Can Change Your Brain," *Psych Central*, last modified May 27, 2019, http://psychcentral.com/blog/words-can-change-your-brain-2/.

13. "You Get What You Pay For? Costly Placebo Works Better Than Cheaper One," *ScienceDaily*, March 5, 2008, http://www.sciencedaily.com/releases/2008/03/080304173339.htm.

RICKY KALMON

Visionary Architect in Personal Growth

RICKY KALMON is a mindset expert, motivational speaker, and celebrity hypnotist who delivers high-energy and motivational keynote programs. His programs are inspirational and offer compelling, applicable tools anyone can use in personal and professional development. Kalmon reveals how our mindset can be the greatest tool in achieving new heights, reducing stress, and increasing productivity and potential.

Ricky Kalmon's mindset message and techniques will change the way you live, work, and think. Kalmon works with Fortune 500 companies, sales teams, leaders, executives, and sports teams, teaching them how to reinforce their thoughts and beliefs to enhance their results. By creating awareness of your thoughts, Kalmon reveals how to enhance your mindset to eliminate doubt and ignite your positive intentions. Through his programs, thousands have changed their world by changing the way they think.

Benefits of Ricky Kalmon's programs include:

› Stress reduction/ mindfulness

› Overcoming challenges/ adapting to change

› Increasing accountability and potential

› Reinforcing confidence/ attitude and belief

› Igniting purpose and prosperity

As an international speaker, motivator, and success expert, Ricky will take you and your organization to the next level of success. For more information visit: www.rickykalmon.com

Ricky Kalmon can be heard on his podcast, **Amplify Your Mindset**. Each episode features business leaders, motivators, and incredible individuals who share how mindset has contributed to their success by helping them overcome challenges, make transitions, remove doubt and fear, and push themselves to exceed their own expectations. Available on iTunes, Google Play, Spotify, and iHeartRadio.

---

www.rickykalmon.com
Corporate programs that leverage
mindset and inspire growth!

AUDIO SUPPORT
PROGRAM

This book comes with an audio support program for each chapter. Download the Ricky Kalmon app by visiting **rickykalmon.com/app** or scanning the QR code provided below. Once you download it, you will have access to the Leverage Your Mindset Audio Support Program that I have created exclusively for this book. Use the password **RKMINDSET** to claim this exclusive content. After each chapter, there will be instructions on which audio track to listen to. Please listen only to the track correlated with each day's activities and instructions.

www.soundwisdom.com